FORCE DRAWDOWN

A USAF PHOTO HISTORY 1988-1995

RENÉ J. FRANCILLON
WITH JIM DUNN & CARL E. PORTER

Schiffer Military/Aviation History
Atglen, PA

Above: McDonnell Douglas F-15E Eagle of the 335th FS, 4th Wing, Air Combat Command during the Gunsmoke '93 competition. (Jim Dunn)

Front cover photo: Lockheed SR-71A (64-17976) of the 1st SRS, 9th SRW, Strategic Air Command, during a refueling training sortie on 28 September 1989, four months before Blackbirds were retired. (René J. Francillon)

Rear cover photo: McDonnell Douglas F-15C Eagle of the 57th FS, Air Combat Command, on 24 June 1992. (René J. Francillon)

Book Design by René Francillon and Robert Biondi.

Copyright © 1995 by René Francillon, Jim Dunn & Carl E. Porter.
Library of Congress Catalog Number: 94-73929

Printed in Hong Kong
ISBN: 0-88740-777-3

We are interested in hearing from authors with book ideas on related topics.

Published by Schiffer Publishing Ltd.
77 Lower Valley Road
Atglen, PA 19310
Please write for a free catalog.
This book may be purchased from the publisher.
Please include $2.95 postage.
Try your bookstore first.

FACING A NEW WORLD

In military vernacular, an impossible task is frequently described as "trying to put ten pounds of manure in a five-pound bag." This bit of barracks philosophy adequately characterizes the predicament in which the USAF has been placed by a steady dose of force reduction coupled with the infusion of a broader range of responsibilities. Between January 1988 and February 1994, the number of operational aircraft has been reduced by more than 22 per cent while during the approximate same period personnel strength dropped over 26 per cent. Notwithstanding this significant force drawdown, the Air Force, since its decisive contribution to swift victory in the Gulf War, has seen its activities multiply. Not only does it carry on its usual defense and training activities, including numerous exercises in the United States and abroad, but it also monitors and intercepts illegal drug traffic and participates in several operations overseas. Deny Flight and Provide Promise in Bosnia-Herzegovina; Provide Comfort and Southern Watch in Southwest Asia; Provide Relief, Restore Hope, and Continue Hope in Somalia; and Restore Democracy in Haiti, as well as a weary watch over developments in North Korea have seen, and continue to see, men and women of the Air Force stretch their endurance near to the limit. Yet, outside of the military, few are those who realize that drastic reductions have already gutted USAF aircraft inventory and personnel strength while many are those who call for further reductions.

In January 1988, at the beginning of the eighth year of the Reagan administration, the United States Air Force had some 9,300 operational aircraft. Like the other services, it was starting to reap benefits from rising military budgets. A series of multi-year contracts was assuring rapid replacement of obsolete combat aircraft, military airlift aircraft, and helicopters.

Using the Nation's most powerful non-lethal weapon – the strength of the world's largest economy – President Reagan had launched a determined offensive against the 'Evil Empire.' Military modernization and development (or at least the threat of development) of the Strategic Defense Initiative placed the Soviet Union in front of an economically impossible task. For the American economy, the price of this offensive – rising budget deficit and decreasing strength of the dollar – was high. That price, however, was small compared to that which would have been incurred to fight World War III against an unrepentant Soviet Union. Moreover, these sacrifices did win the Cold War and freed the Nation and most of the world from the constant fear of nuclear holocaust.

Imperceptibly at first, the undeclared economic war brought about momentous changes. In March 1985, immediately after succeeding hard-line Konstantin Chernenko as General Secretary of the Communist Party, Mikhail Gorbachev agreed to a new round of U.S.-Soviet arms reduction negotiations. Subsequently, no doubt prodded by knowledge that strengthening of U.S. forces and American development of new weapons (notably, SDI, B-2 stealth bomber, and Seawolf submarines) could not be matched or countered without investments far beyond Soviet capability, Gorbachev launched *Perestroika* and *Glasnost.* Few were those then realizing the speed at which the Soviet Union and the Warsaw Pact were about to collapse.

In Germany, the Berlin Wall fell in November 1989, the withdrawal of Soviet forces followed, and reunification occurred in October 1990. Further east, the Warsaw Pact military alliance was dissolved in February 1991, the Baltic states (Estonia, Latvia, and Lithuania) regained their independence in September 1991, and the Soviet Union disintegrated and was replaced by the loosely held together Commonwealth of Independent States in December 1991. The Cold War had been won.

Even before the fall of the Berlin Wall or the collapse of the Soviet Union, U.S. military build-up was slowed down. Military budgets began to drop in 1989 (both in current dollars and in constant dollars, as well as a percentage of U.S. gross domestic product) and USAF personnel, which had reached a decade high of 608,200 in 1986, began a steady decrease (to an estimated 425,700 in 1994). The executive and legislative branches of government were losing no time in extracting a peace dividend for taxpayers.

Defeat of a New Bully and the Emergence of a New World Order
While the Cold War was about to be won, the United States suddenly had to face a new reality. On 2 August 1990, Iraqi forces invaded Kuwait, prompting President Bush to commit forces to stop aggression and ultimately, under the sponsorship of the United Nations, regain freedom for the Kuwaiti population. Already having seen its strength reduced from its peak during the preceding decade, the Air Force, along with other services and soon after allied forces, lost no time in deploying to Southwest Asia. The Desert Shield build-up and Desert Storm victory have been dealt with adequately in numerous books and further detailing fall outside the scope of this book. Suffice it to say, that, notwithstanding the overwhelming demonstration of air power, most of which was provided by the USAF, Desert Shield and Desert Storm also brought to light shortcomings due in part to the previously initiated force reduction.

Unfortunately, the euphoria which followed the Coalition victory precluded immediate remedial of these shortcomings and led to further force reduction at a pace defying reason. Budget and personnel strength proceeded on their downward spiral at an accelerated pace. Congress, intent on reaping the maximum peace dividend, failed to provide adequate funding for critically needed hardware (e.g., new Suppression of Enemy Air Defenses aircraft as replacements for weary and difficult to maintain F-4Gs and EF-111As, C-141B replacements, and tactical reconnaissance assets). Meanwhile, politics, without as well as within the Air Force, appears to have had more to do in shaping the new force than had sound strategic and tactical considerations in time of shrinking budgets.

Costly Cosmetic
Thus, at a time when Air Force personnel strength is being drastically reduced and a dwindling number of operational flight crews and wrench benders are stretched out to their limits by frequent deployments to support operations in far-flung places, there appears to be no shortage of officers and enlisted personnel at the Pentagon, and at headquarters of major commands and field operating agencies, to dream up costly cosmetic changes with little or questionable operational benefits.

With the significant reduction in Soviet nuclear threat and the increasing reliance on bombers for conventional missions, merging Tactical Air Command and

Strategic Air Command into a single entity was a sound decision. Its implementation was perhaps not as wisely achieved and certainly did not do much to improve morale. Needing an insignia for the new Air Combat Command, the powers that be retained the sword of Tactical Air Command, not the shield of Strategic Air Command. Soon bombers, strategic reconnaissance aircraft, and some tankers sprouted TAC-style tail codes and the milky way fuselage stripe of SAC faded into oblivion. For former SAC personnel the writing was clearly to be seen. More than any others they had helped prevent the Cold War from turning into a nuclear disaster, but it was their TAC brethren which were to reap the benefits of a new world order.

Having succeeded to TAC and absorbed SAC, Air Combat Command no longer felt the need for differentiating between fighter interceptors and tactical fighters. FIS, FIG, FIW, TFS, TFG, and TFW designations were logically replaced by FS, FG, and FW. However, was it necessary to spend the money to replace immediately unit stationery, building signs, flight suit patches, and aircraft decals? Moreover, if the FS designation is appropriate for squadrons flying F-15s or F-16s, it remains out of place when applied to units flying A-10s or F-111s. In its quest for logic, ACC missed the opportunity to tie these units with the traditions of USAAF units which flew A-20s, A-24s, and A-35s in World War II or those of USAF units which flew A-1s and B-26s in more recent time.

Conversely, in their pursuit of a new image ACC planners did not replace the fighter designation with that of "persoot," even though this would have been in keeping with the move to transfer the lineage and traditions of old units (including Pursuit Squadrons of the Air Service and Army Air Corps) to the fast dwindling number of units left in the active force. Wisely, they have transferred unit designators of inactivated units with long and glorious histories to surviving units with a shorter and less active past. However, in some cases, politics played a greater role than a keen desire to preserve history. Both the 20th Fighter Wing and the 363d Reconnaissance Wing had been established in July 1947, but the 20th only saw action against Libya in 1986 and during the Gulf War in 1991 while the 363d took part in the Cuban missile crisis of 1962, supported operations in Southeast Asia during the 1960s and early 1970s, and was back in action during the Gulf War. Yet, the Shaw AFB unit has been renumbered 20th Fighter Wing to honor the unit to which the Air Force Chief of Staff had been assigned early in his career. One more case of stationery having to be reprinted, signs repainted, patches ordered, and decals applied. Let us celebrate by wearing our new 'bus driver' dress uniform!

Not to be outdone, as successor to Military Airlift Command, Air Mobility Command felt compelled to introduce changes for the mere satisfaction of adopting a new image. Military was dropped from MAS, MAG, and MAW designations, these units becoming simply Airlift Squadrons/Groups/Wings. In addition, squadrons were to be renumbered consecutively within a wing. (For example, in early 1994, after the 7th, 75th, and 86th Airlift Squadrons had been renumbered, the 60th Airlift Wing was made up of the 19th through 22d Airlift Squadrons. Renumbering the 7th and the 86th did little to extend the life of their now marginally useful C-141Bs.) Again, expenses for decals, patches, signs, and stationery were unmatched by gains in efficiency or morale.

Back to the Future

The USAF reorganization which followed the Gulf War, and was intended to adapt it to changing requirements stemming from a new world order, led to numerous cases of 'reinventing the wheel.' In the light of historical precedents, some of these changes are questionable.

Anticipating the need to deploy small but closely integrated forces to respond to localized threats, Air Combat Command, Pacific Air Forces, and US Air Forces in Europe set out to organize composite or air intervention wings. Whereas most USAF wings had since 1947 been made up of two to four squadrons equipped with a single type of aircraft, these new wings were conceived as mini air forces with each of their squadrons equipped with different types of aircraft. For example, ACC's 366th Wing at Mountain Home AFB, Idaho, currently includes a squadron of F-15Cs for air superiority (the 390th FS), a squadron of F-16Cs for battlefield support (the 389th FS), a squadron of F-15Es for deep strike (the 391st FS), a squadron of B-1Bs for heavy strike (the 34th BS operating from Ellsworth AFB, South Dakota), and a squadron of KC-135Rs for air refueling (the 22d AREFS). Furthermore, for specific deployments the 366th Wing would be supplemented by detachments of F-4Gs, EF-111A, E-3s, and C-130s drawn from other wings.

While in theory such a self-contained mini air force has merits, lessons from the past raise doubts on its effectiveness. In 1944, the USAAF had organized three air commando groups consisting of a headquarters plus fighter, bomber, liaison, and troop carrier squadrons flying P-51s and P-47s, B-25s, L-1s and L-5s, C-47s, UC-64s, and CG-4 and TG-5 gliders. These three groups distinguished themselves during operations, often from temporary fields behind enemy lines, in the CBI theater of operations and in the Philippines. However, problems associated with spares provisioning and maintenance of small number of aircraft of different types proved the source of much difficulties and the concept was dropped after the war ended. One can only wonder if spares provisioning and maintenance requirements for aircraft as diverse as F-15s and B-1s, which certainly are much more complex than WWII vintage aircraft, will prove any easier for the 366th Wing and other similar air intervention wings.

Similarly forgetting lessons from the past, the Air Force has transferred its C-130 tactical transports from Air Mobility Command to ACC, PACAF, and USAFE (the reverse had taken place in 1974-75 when Military Airlift Command had gained control over tactical transports from TAC, PACAF, and USAFE). In the same vein, the Air Force is again having most operational training on combat aircraft conducted under the aegis of its training command (Air Education and Training Command). That approach had been found wanting during the 1950s and SAC, TAC, and MATS gained control of operational training from ATC. Will it work this time?

Closing Bases

As residents of many areas are only too aware, force drawdown has not just been a case of reducing aircraft inventory by phasing out and not replacing older types. Neither has it been limited to reducing active duty, reserve, guard or civilian personnel through normal attrition or by providing incentives for early retirement. It has also meant closing Air Force installations in the United States, its possessions, and abroad. Between Fiscal Year 1986 and Fiscal Year 1995, the number of major installations has been reduced from 139 to 94. Closed, or about to be closed, are such major bases in the United States or its possessions as Bergstrom, Blytheville, Carswell, Castle, Chanute, England, George, Griffiss, Loring, Lowry, Mather, Myrtle Beach, Norton, Pease, Plattsburgh, Wheeler, Williams, and Wurtsmith. Others, such as March, Grissom, Homestead, and Rickenbacker, have been or will be reduced to reserve status. On Guam, Andersen AFB no longer has operational units permanently assigned. Major operational bases overseas which have closed include Clark in the Philippines; Soesterberg in the Netherlands; Torrejon in Spain; Alconbury, Bentwaters, and Upper Heyford in the United Kingdom; and Bitburg, Hahn, Sembach, and Zweibrücken in Germany. All indications are that under the next BRAC phase, the number of bases which will close will increase dramatically.

It is most unlikely that bases which have closed, aircraft which have been prematurely phased down, units which have been deactivated, and personnel which have been furloughed will ever serve their Nation again. The following pictorial history is a tribute to the dedicated men and women who served in the United States Air Force and a sad farewell to aircraft and bases which helped win the Cold War.

USAF AIRCRAFT INVENTORY
(excluding aircraft stored at AMARC or elsewhere)

AIRCRAFT TYPES	31 Jan 88	31 Jan 93	28 Feb 94
Vought A-7			
A-7D	342	36	0
A-7K	30	4	0
Fairchild-Republic A-10			
A-10A	631	299	251
OA-10A	22	109	133
Cessna A-37			
NA-37B	3	2	0
OA-37B	82	2	0
Rockwell B-1			
B-1B	86	96	95
Northrop B-2			
B-2A	0	5	7
Boeing B-52			
NB-52B (loan to NASA)	1	1	1
B-52G	167	41	2
B-52H	96	95	95
Lockheed C-5			
C-5A	77	76	74
C-5B	24	50	50
C-5C	0	0	2
McDonnell Douglas C-9			
C-9A	20	20	20
C-9C	3	3	3
McDonnell Douglas KC-10			
KC-10A	57	59	59
Beech C-12			
C-12A	29	0	0
C-12C	0	27	27
C-12D	6	6	6
C-12F	46	46	45
C-12J	6	6	6
McDonnell Douglas C-17			
C-17A	0	5	11
Boeing C-18			
C-18A	2	0	0
C-18B	0	1	1
EC-18B	5	4	4
EC-18D	0	2	2
Gulfstream C-20			
C-20A	3	3	3
C-20B	7	7	7
C-20C	3	3	3
Gates Learjet C-21			
C-21A	83	83	83
Boeing C-22			
C-22A	1	1	0
C-22B	4	4	4
Shorts C-23			
C-23A	18	3	3
Boeing C-25			
VC-25A	0	2	2
Fairchild C-26			
C-26A	0	11	11
C-26B	0	16	22
UC-26C	0	1	1
Alenia/CTAS C-27			
C-27A	0	10	10
Lockheed C-130			
C-130A	71	24	0
NC-130A	0	1	1
C-130B	93	29	11
NC-130B	0	1	1
C-130E	276	280	268
C-130H	152	226	229
LC-130H	4	4	4
NC-130H	1	1	2
Lockheed AC-130			
AC-130A	10	10	10
AC-130H	10	9	9
AC-130U	0	3	3
Lockheed EC-130			
EC-130E	15	15	15
EC-130H	15	15	15
Lockheed HC-130			
HC-130H	25	0	0
HC-130N	15	17	18
HC-130P	17	38	38
Lockheed MC-130			
MC-130E	14	14	14
MC-130H	0	13	21
Lockheed WC-130			
WC-130E	6	6	1
WC-130H	14	6	10
Convair C-131			
C-131B	2	0	0
C-131D	8	0	0
C-131E	2	0	0
NC-131H	1	0	0

AIRCRAFT TYPES	31 Jan 88	31 Jan 93	28 Feb 94
Boeing C-135			
C-135A	2	2	1
NC-135A	1	0	0
C-135B	5	4	3
C-135C	3	2	2
C-135E	3	3	3
Boeing EC-135			
EC-135A	5	3	0
EC-135B	1	0	0
EC-135C	13	11	9
EC-135E	4	4	4
EC-135G	4	0	0
EC-135H	5	0	0
EC-135J	4	1	0
EC-135K	2	2	2
EC-135L	5	0	0
EC-135N	1	1	1
EC-135P	3	0	0
EC-135Y	1	1	1
Boeing KC-135			
KC-135A	333	68	11
NKC-135A	9	6	1
KC-135D	4	4	4
KC-135E	136	159	159
NKC-135E	1	2	2
KC-135Q	54	54	46
KC-135R	101	313	335
KC-135T	0	0	8
Boeing RC-135 & TC-135			
TC-135B	0	0	1
RC-135S	2	2	2
TC-135S	1	1	1
RC-135U	2	2	2
RC-135V	8	8	8
RC-135W	6	6	6
TC-135W	0	1	1
RC-135X	0	1	1
Boeing OC-135 & WC-135			
OC-135B	0	0	1
WC-135B	7	7	3
Boeing C-137			
C-137B	3	3	3
C-137C	4	4	4
EC-137D	0	1	1
Lockheed C-140			
C-140A	4	0	0
C-140B	6	0	0
Lockheed C-141			
C-141A	1	0	0
NC-141A	3	4	4
C-141B	267	263	244
Boeing E-3			
E-3A	9	0	0
E-3B	17	24	24
E-3C	8	10	10
Boeing E-4			
E-4B	4	4	4
Boeing/Grumman E-8			
E-8A	0	2	2
de Havilland Canada E-9			
E-9A	0	2	2
McDonnell F-4			
F-4C	70	0	0
NF-4C	4	0	0
F-4D	391	0	0
NF-4D	3	0	0
F-4E	402	24	16
NF-4E	9	0	0
QF-4E	0	4	4
YF-4E	1	0	0
F-4G	102	105	61
QF-4G	0	2	1
McDonnell RF-4			
RF-4C	318	94	47
NRF-4C	2	0	0
QRF-4C	0	2	2
Northrop F-5			
F-5E	84	0	0
F-5F	7	0	0
McDonnell Douglas F-15			
F-15A	311	193	164
YF-15A	4	3	3
F-15B	52	38	35
YF-15B	2	2	2
F-15C	369	364	361
F-15D	60	55	54
F-15E	2	183	197
General Dynamics F-16			
F-16A	365	573	433
NF-16A	1	1	1
YF-16A	3	0	0
F-16B	109	107	93
YF-16B	2	0	0
F-16C	420	962	1,050
F-16D	30	166	183

AIRCRAFT TYPES	31 Jan 88	31 Jan 93	28 Feb 94
Lockheed F-22			
YF-22A	0	1	1
North American F-100			
F-100D	19	1	0
QF-100D	60	1	0
F-100F	2	0	0
QF-100F	3	0	0
Convair F-106			
F-106A	18	0	0
QF-106A	5	102	90
F-106B	5	2	0
QF-106B	2	4	21
General Dynamics F-111			
F-111A	44	1	0
NF-111A	1	0	0
F-111D	82	0	0
F-111E	80	65	26
F-111F	85	82	81
F-111G	0	19	0
General Dynamics/Grumman EF-111			
EF-111A	42	40	40
General Dynamics FB-111			
FB-111A	62	0	0
Lockheed F-117			
YF-117A	3	0	0
F-117A	45	56	55
Schweizer TG-7			
TG-7A	7	9	9
Bell H-1			
UH-1F	12	0	0
HH-1H	29	25	25
UH-1N	69	67	66
Sikorsky H-3			
CH-3E	31	0	0
HH-3E	46	9	9
Sikorsky H-53			
CH-53A	0	12	0
NCH-53A	0	2	2
TH-53A	0	1	6
HH-53B	4	0	0
CH-53C	8	0	0
HH-53C	21	0	0
MH-53H	8	0	0
MH-53J	0	41	41
Sikorsky H-60			
HH-60A	1	0	0
UH-60A	11	0	0
HH-60G	0	52	82
MH-60G	7	23	13
UH-60L	0	21	1
Cessna O-2			
O-2A	3	0	0
O-2B	2	2	0
Lockheed SR-71			
SR-71A	19	0	0
SR-71B	1	0	0
Beech T-1			
T-1A	0	28	65
Slingsby T-3			
T-3A	0	0	4
Lockheed T-33			
T-33A	40	0	0
NT-33A	1	1	1
Cessna T-37			
T-37B	604	538	530
OT-37B	29	0	0
Northrop T-38			
T-38A	697	670	553
AT-38B	113	45	66
North American T-39			
T-39A	3	0	0
CT-39A	2	1	0
NT-39A	1	3	3
T-39B	6	5	4
Cessna T-41			
T-41A	50	31	0
T-41C	48	48	48
T-41D	2	2	2
Boeing T-43			
T-43A	19	12	12
CT-43A	0	7	3
Lockheed TR-1 & U-2			
TR-1A	21	0	0
TR-1B	2	0	0
U-2R	7	20	19
U-2R(T)	1	3	3
de Havilland Canada U-6			
U-6A	1	0	0
Rockwell OV-10			
OV-10A	79	0	0
de Havilland Canada UV-18			
UV-18B	3	2	2
TOTAL OPERATIONAL INVENTORY	**9,303**	**7,763**	**7,219**

In January 1988, 17 A-7Ds and two A-7Ks were still assigned to 2724 Det DT for use in training F-117A pilots of the 4450th Tactical Group. Coded LV, these aircraft operated from Nellis AFB and the Tonopah Test Range Facility. (René J. Francillon)

69-14582, the first A-7D-1-CV for the USAF, became one of the last A-7Ds operated by the Air Force Flight Test Center at Edwards AFB. All A-7s were withdrawn from service with active duty units before January 1993. (Carl E. Porter)

A-7D of the 175th TFS, 114th TFG, South Dakota ANG, at the Boise Air Terminal, Idaho, on 17 July 1988. The 'store' beneath the starboard wing is a spare main wheel. (René J. Francillon)

Snow is gently falling as this A-7D sits on the ramp at night while personnel of the 146th TFS, 112th TFG, Pennsylvania ANG, undergo ORI at Phelps Collins ANGB, Michigan, in October 1989. (Sgt. John Lombardo, PA ANG)

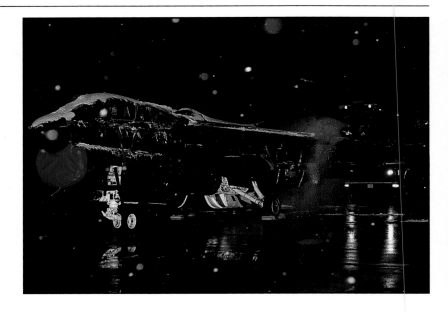

Carrying a Maverick missile beneath its port wing, 70-1023, an A-7D of the 120th TFS, 140th TFW, stands ready for a training sortie from Buckley ANGB in May 1991. The Colorado ANG unit converted to F-16Cs shortly afterward. (Robert B. Greby)

The 112th FS, 178th FG, Ohio ANG, was the last USAF unit to fly A-7s. At the beginning of 1993, the ANG still possessed 36 A-7Ds and four A-7Ks. A few months later all had been withdrawn. (René J. Francillon)

Just weeks before the New Mexico ANG converted to F-16Cs, these three A-7Ds (70-1034, 72-0225, and 75-0386) of the 188th FS, 150th FG, were photographed on 20 May 1992 during an air refueling sortie over the Winslow track in Arizona. (René J. Francillon)

A-7 training was last provided for the Air National Guard by the 195th TFTS, 162d TFG. The Arizona ANG unit ended A-7D/K operations on 26 July 1991, 26 months after this A-7K crew was photographed departing from the ramp at the Tucson IAP for a training sortie over the Barry M. Goldwater Bombing and Gunnery Range. (René J. Francillon)

Back from a gunnery training sortie, this A-7K belongs to the 125th TFS, 138th TFG. This OK ANG unit became the penultimate Guard squadron to fly Corsair IIs and converted to F-16Cs in 1993. (Douglas D. Olson)

Periodic depot maintenance for A-10As and OA-10As of the USAF and its reserve components is performed at the Sacramento Air Logistics Center, McClellan AFB, California. Immediately after the Gulf War, when this photograph was taken, SM-ALC was busy. This Air Logistics Center is now fighting for survival and McClellan AFB may well become one of the next bases to close. (Jim Dunn)

Lacking the glamor of supersonic fighters, the A-10 has long been unloved. Its performance during the Gulf War earned it much praise, but failed to prevent the number of operational aircraft from being drastically reduced. (Jim Dunn)

Like so many USAF units, the Nellis AFB wing has gone through several redesignations in the last few years. On 1 October 1991, it was redesignated from 57th Fighter Weapons Wing to 57th Fighter Wing and on 1 April 1993 it became simply the 57th Wing. It was the 57th FWW when one of its A-10As (81-0945) was caught struggling to get airborne on its way to the Nellis Range on a hot June 1991 afternoon. (René J. Francillon)

The 23d TFW, heir of the 'Flying Tigers' of World War II fame, operated A-10s from England AFB between 1980 and 1993. Following the closure of this Louisiana base, the 23d Wing has been reorganized as a composite wing at Pope AFB, North Carolina, with two squadrons of C-130Es, one squadron of F-16C/Ds, one squadron of A/OA-10As, and one squadron of EC-130Es (based at Keesler AFB, MS). Full head-on view of a 23d TFW 'Warthog' emphasizes tiger markings, 'can opener' gun, offset nose gear, and Pave Penny designator. (Carl E. Porter)

W. K. Kellog Airport, Battle Creek, 6 August 1994: A pair of A-10As from the 172d FS, 110th FG, Michigan ANG, at 'last chance' before a training sortie. (Carl E. Porter)

The Shaw AFB wing was a tactical reconnaissance unit until October 1981. Equipped mostly with F-16s but retaining a squadron of RF-4Cs, it then became the 363d Tactical Fighter Wing. It disposed of its recce Phantoms in September 1989 and, renamed 363d FW, had added A-10As by the time this Warthog was photographed in October 1993. It has now been renumbered as the 20th FW. (Jim Dunn)

Beauty on a beast. Almost as if A-10 maintenance crews were ashamed of the warts of the Warthog, nose art has frequently been painted inconspicuously on the inside of the access door beneath the cockpit on the port side. Notably, this was the case of the luscious redhead adorning 77-0245, an A-10A of the 45th TFS, AFRES. (Jim Dunn)

Even though it is extremely effective against armor, the potent 30-mm GAU-8 cannon is not the preferred weapon of the A-10A as its effective range requires that the aircraft be flown within reach of most ground weapons. Hence, Maverick missiles have become the weapons of choice for tank busting. (René J. Francillon)

Warthogs were first assigned to the Alaska Air Command in October 1981 when the 18th TFS, 343d Composite Wing, at Eielson AFB was equipped with A-10As. Current Warthog operator in Alaska is the 355th FS, 354th FW, PACAF, flying OA-10As. (Carl E. Porter)

So big as to look almost like pontoons, stores beneath the wing of this OA-10A (79-0179) of the 55th FS, 20th FW, are 600-gallon tanks. The scuttlebutt has it that the early 1994 renumbering of the Shaw AFB unit from 363d to 20th Fighter Wing was a not too subtle ploy to get on the good side of the outgoing USAF Chief of Staff who, early in his career, had been assigned to the USAFE wing at RAF Upper Heyford. (Jim Dunn)

Carrying empty LAU-68 rocket pods, 77-0207, an OA-10A of the 23d TASS, 602d TAIRCW, lands at Nellis AFB on 5 June 1991. Three months later, the 602d Tactical Air Control Wing was redesignated 602d Air Control Wing. It was inactivated in April 1992. (René J. Francillon)

OA-10A (80-0283) of the 25th Fighter Squadron, 51st Wing, at Misawa AB, Japan, on 13 September 1992. Along with the other flying components of the 51st Wing – the 36th FS with F-16C/Ds, the 38th RQS with HH-60Gs, and the 55th ALF with C-21As – this PACAF squadron is based at Osan AB, Korea. (Masanori Ogawa)

Bearing the serial number 70-1310, this NA-37B was still assigned to the 412th Test Wing at Edwards AFB in February 1994. By then it had accummulated 5,292 flight hours. (René J. Francillon)

In June 1991, prior to converting to F-16 A/B ADFs and being redesignated 168th FS, 182d FG, the 168th TASS took part for a last time in an Air Warrior exercise. The Illinois ANG flew out its last OA-37Bs on 3 June 1992. (René J. Francillon)

The 110th TASS, 111th TASG, Pennsylvania ANG, flew OA-37Bs for seven years. It completed conversion to OA-10As in December 1989. (Carl E. Porter)

84-0055, a Lancer of the 96th Bomb Wing, still carried 'Sunrise Surprise' nose art when visiting McClellan AFB on 25 May 1991. Briefly designated 96th Wing, the Dyess AFB unit is now the 7th Wing. (Jim Dunn)

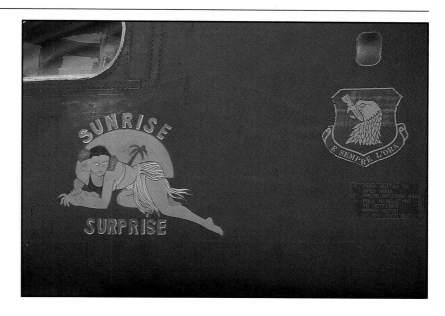

Wings swept forward, B-1B taxies under the tower at Edwards AFB. Lancer achieved IOC with the 337th BS, 96th BW, in September 1986. By 28 February 1994, the high-time B-1B – 85-0072 of the 7th BW – had flown 2,697 hours. (Carl E. Porter)

A B-1B of the 46th BS, 319th BW, takes-off from runway 3 Left at Nellis AFB during the Gunsmoke '93 competition. The wing was scheduled to lose its B-1Bs less than one year later. (Jim Dunn)

Late afternoon sun highlights the camouflage of a B-1B as it returns from a sortie over the Nellis range complex on 24 June 1992. (René J. Francillon)

Contrary to appearances, and notwithstanding its less than smooth operational career, the B-1B has not yet been relegated to pylon display status. This 28th Bomb Wing aircraft was caught climbing in front of the Nellis AFB tower during a Red Flag exercise in February 1993. (René J. Francillon)

At the beginning of 1993, two squadrons of the 28th Bomb Wing (the 37th BS and 77th BS) shared 27th B-1Bs. Underside view emphasizes power plant installation and shows location of two bomb bays. (Jim Dunn)

Framed against a stormy cloud as it is about to land, the B-2 takes on a particularly sinister appearance. Designed to provide the Air Force with a nuclear weapons system capable of penetrating Soviet air defenses with a high probability of success, the B-2 is now seen as an effective method of projecting conventional strength against lesser, but nevertheless sophisticated, adversaries. (Northrop Grumman)

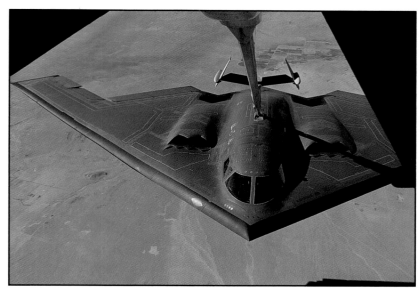

Just as had been the case with the SR-71, the B-2 is particularly spectacular when viewed in its element. Conversely, in side profiles on the ground, as most of us get to see them, both the SR-71 and the B-2 are less inspiring. (Northrop Grumman)

The price tag for a single squadron of B-2s, plus pipeline aircraft, is exceedingly high. In view of current and anticipated threats, would we not have been better off spending the same amount to acquire several squadrons of F-15Es? (USAF)

Bailed out to NASA, but still carried in the USAF inventory, the oldest Stratofortress is this NB-52B (52-0008). Due to its specialized utilization, this aircraft had only been flown 1,885 hours by the end of February 1994. (Carl E. Porter)

Painted in SIOP camouflage scheme, this 93d Bomb Wing B-52G drops away from the tanker on its way to Tinker AFB where it was to undergo PDM at the Oklahoma City Air Logistics Center. (René J. Francillon)

Slowed down by its drag chute to almost a standstill, this B-52G of the 93d Bomb Wing is about to exit runway 31. Colors are enhanced by the almost horizontal rays of the sun at the end of a sunny winter day at Castle AFB. (René J. Francillon)

'Old Crow Express,' a B-52G-85-BW (57-6492) from the 397th Bomb Wing at Wurstmith AFB, Michigan, was deployed to King Abdul Aziz IAP, Jeddah, Saudi Arabia, prior to Desert Storm. Fifty-one bombs are painted on the lower port side of the fuselage, indicating that this Buff may have flown that many sorties against Iraqi forces – an almost incredible achievement as combat operations started on 17 January and ended on 28 February. (Michael Gruenenfelder)

Last wing to be assigned B-52s was the 366th Wing. Not based with the other squadrons at Mountain Home AFB, Idaho, the 34th BS was at Castle AFB to enable its B-52Gs to be maintained alongside those of the 93d Bomb Wing. Still assigned to the 366th Wing, the 34th has now transferred to Ellsworth AFB, South Dakota, to fly B-1Bs. Bearing the tail code MO of the 366th, 57-6520 was photographed on final approach at Castle AFB on 2 November 1992. (René J. Francillon)

First wing to be equipped with B-52s, the 93d Bomb Wing ended nearly 29 years of Buff operations in style as in October 1993, a few months before being deactivated, it took top bomber honors during Gunsmoke '93 at Nellis AFB, Nevada. (Jim Dunn)

Some of the best nose art applied to Buffs were markings painted by Derrel Fleener to B-52Gs of the 320th Bomb Wing at Mather AFB, California. Honoring Gen MacArthur, 'Old Soldier' was a B-52G-95-BW (58-0178) of the 441st BS. (Jim Dunn)

For the naval attack mission, a number of B-52Gs were modified to carry 12 AGM-84 Harpoon antiship missiles on two Heavy Store Adapter Beams (HSAB), one under each wing between the fuselage and the inboard engine nacelles. (René J. Francillon)

The 92d Bomb Wing at Fairchild AFB, Washington, flew Buffs between 1957 and 1994. The tragic end of one of its last B-52Hs in June 1994 was played again and again on national TV, with most commentators proving once more that newscasters have a dismal knowledge of aviation and military operations. (Christian Jacquet)

Based at Carswell AFB, Texas, the 7th Bomb Wing first received B-52Fs in 1958 and converted to B-52Ds ten years later. It flew B-52Hs between 1982 and 1993. Photographed in July 1988, B-52H-170-BW (61-0026) was assigned to the 92d Bomb Wing at Fairchild AFB when Carswell AFB closed. (Carl E. Porter)

Photographed at Fairchild AFB on Bastille Day 1988 (a rather appropriate occasion when considering that the photographer is a Frog) when it served with the 92d Bomb Wing, B-52H-170-BW (61-0022) became one of the first five Buffs assigned to AFRES. On 28 February 1994, by which time it had flown 13,189 hours, it was assigned to the 93d BS at Barksdale AFB, Louisiana. (Christian Jacquet)

61-0033, an aircraft from the last production batch – B-52H-175-BW – on final approach at Nellis AFB, Nevada, on 15 March 1990. Rainbow fin markings are those of the 410th Bomb Wing. After flying B-52Hs for just over 31 years, the K. I. Sawyer AFB unit was inactivated in 1994 as this Michigan base was joining the long list of base closures. (René J. Francillon)

Still wearing the 'white top' scheme in which C-5As went into service, this Galaxy belongs to the 60th Military Airlift Wing. Military was dropped from the designation of C-5 and C-141 wings, groups, and squadrons, in June 1992 when Air Mobility Command was organized to succeed to Military Airlift Command. (Carl E. Porter)

Whether serving with active duty wings (60th AW & 436th AW), AFRES associate wings (349th AW & 512th AW), AFRES squadrons with their own aircraft (68th AS & 337th AS), or the only ANG squadron flying C-5s (137th AS), Galaxy crews get regularly requalified for air refueling. Here a Travis-based C-5A (69-0027) flies alongside the Oregon coast on 8 November 1993 as pilots of the 60th AW trade seats with pilots of the 349th AW before taking on more fuel during a training sortie. (René J. Francillon)

Flying Cessna O-2s since 1971, the New York ANG's 105th Tactical Air Support Group was selected to become the first ANG unit to fly heavy lift aircraft. Initially, it was planned to equip the 105th Military Airlift Group with Boeing C-19As (designation set aside for used Boeing 747s which Congress wanted the Air Force to buy from airlines with excess capacity). In the end, however, reason prevailed and in July 1985 the 105th Airlift Group received its first C-5A. (Douglas D. Olson)

Repainted in the current AMC grey scheme, this C-5B (84-0062) doing touch-and-go's at Travis AFB on 6 May 1993 wears the tail band identifying aircraft maintained for the 60th Airlift Wing by the 22d AMU. (René J. Francillon)

Framed against Mt Rainier, a C-5A (68-0220) of the 433d AW, AFRES, taxies on runway 34 at the start of a sortie during the Rodeo '94 competition at McChord AFB during the last week in June 1994. (René J. Francillon)

Designed to carry oversize Army equipment, including main battle tanks and CH-47 helicopters, the Galaxy has a voracious appetite. On 22 August 1994, this C-5A (68-0219) of the 439th AW, AFRES, was 'fed' unusual cargo – a Vickers Vimy replica – for airlift from California to England. To fit in the C-5, only the rear fuselage, tail and landing gear of the Vimy had to be removed. The fit, nevertheless, was tight. (René J. Francillon)

With the morning fog of the San Francisco Bay in the background, a C-9A Nightingale taxies in sunshine at Travis AFB. Taken in May 1989, this photograph shows the aircraft with the markings of the 375th Aeromedical Airlift Wing painted on its nose. (René J. Francillon)

Eleven months after 68-8932 had been photographed in the markings of the 375th AAW, 71-0875 was photographed on final to Nellis AFB in the markings of the 375th MAW. This wing is now simply designated 375th AW. Sign painters, patch makers, and stationary printers do not worry about job security as long as they have Air Force contracts! (René J. Francillon)

Photographed on 29 June 1990, this C-9C is one of the 'Congressperson mobile' based at Andrews AFB, Maryland. Initially these aircraft carried the VC-9C designation, but the VIP prefix has since been dropped in a politically correct move to avoid offending taxpayers. (René J. Francillon)

Carrying the markings of the 22d AREFW, 79-1946 has just retracted its gear as it departs Hickam AFB. In Air Force service, KC-10s have racked up an impressive record. (Carl E. Porter)

A KC-10A of the 722d AREFW about to take on fuel from a KC-135E of the 163d ARG, California ANG, on 17 June 1994. Both units are based at 'Tanker Town, USA,' March AFB, but, beginning in September 1994, KC-10As of the 722d ARW were being relocated to Travis AFB and assigned to the newly redesignated 60th Air Mobility Wing along-side C-5A/Bs and C-141Bs (René J. Francillon)

Were it not for reflections from the leading edge of its wing and stabilizers and from its air refueling receptacle, this KC-10A of the 22d ARW in the new AMC scheme would blend effectively with the bleak desert in southeastern California. (René J. Francillon)

Flying over the northern Arabian Gulf, this KC-10A from the 2d Bomb Wing trails its hose in preparation for refueling Navy aircraft during a Desert Storm mission on 21 January 1991. (Rick Morgan)

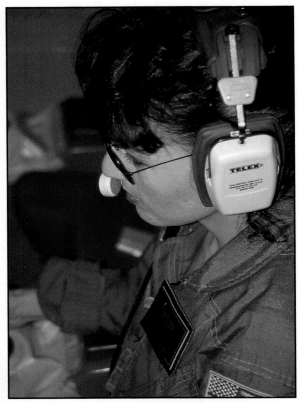

TSgt Celeste Barcelo, a reservist from the 79th AREFS, at her 'office,' the boom operator station of 87-0120, during a refueling sortie in eastern Nevada on 19 May 1993. (René J. Francillon)

Winner of the 1976 ATCA (advanced tanker/cargo aircraft) competition, the KC-10A is truly a dual role aircraft. Here, an AMC crew from the 458th Operations Group at Barksdale AFB is being evaluated as part of the cargo loading competition at McChord AFB during Rodeo '94. (René J. Francillon)

Beech C-12F (84-0167) support aircraft of the 51st Wing at Osan AB, Korea, landing at Yokota AB, Japan, on 29 August 1993. (Masanori Ogawa)

Following the transfer of most tankers from SAC to AMC, Cessna T-37Bs and Northrop T-38As previously assigned to ATC's ACE detachments have been replaced by AMC-owned Beech C-12Fs. 84-0158 is operated as a companion trainer by the 319th Air Refueling Wing at Grand Forks AFB, North Dakota, to provide additional flight experience for its copilots. (René J. Francillon)

In 1987, the National Guard Bureau selected the Fairchild-Swearingen C-26A and the Beech C-12J as ANG Operational Support Turboprop Aircraft (ANGOSTA). Proudly bearing the 'High Rollers' nickname of the Nevada ANG unit, 86-0080 is the C-12J assigned to the 152d Reconnaissance Group at Reno-Cannon IAP. (Carl E. Porter)

First delivered to the 17th AS at Charleston AFB, South Carolina, on Flag Day 1993, the C-17A was scheduled to reach IOC in early 1995. 90-0533 was photographed at McChord AFB on 27 June 1994 during a spirited demonstration (Jim Dunn)

Progress with the C-17A has been excruciatingly slow, initial delays being attributable to the Air Force which selected the McDonnell Douglas design as the winner of the CX competition on 29 August 1981, but did not award the full-scale development contract until 31 December 1985. Additional delays were caused by Congress which did not fund development and production at the required level. Finally, mismanagement by the contractor added further delays. (Carl E. Porter)

If full production is finally authorized, the C-17A is likely to become a worthy replacement for the C-141B. However, development difficulties, program slippage, and cost overrun may well kill an otherwise superb aircraft as Congress, the Air Force, and the contractor point at each other in their search for scapegoats. (René J. Francillon)

At the beginning of 1994, the 4950th Test Wing at Wright-Patterson AFB, Ohio, operated seven ex-707 airliners with C-18 designations. 81-0898 was a C-18B, 81-0891, 81-0892, 81-0894, and 81-0896 were EC-18Bs, and 81-0893 and 81-0895 were C-18Ds. (Jim Dunn)

Right and below: The EC-18Bs are operated in the ARIA (Advanced Range Instrumentation Aircraft) role. Their distinctive nose radome was inherited from that developed in the late sixties for the EC-135N. The three-quarter front view shows the nose of an EC-18B (81-0896) and the front view that of an EC-135N (61-0327). In February 1994, the former was with the 4950th Test Wing at Wright-Patterson AFB, Ohio, while the latter was with the 19th ARW at Robins AFB, Georgia. (Jim Dunn & Peter B. Lewis)

Developed by Gulfstream Aerospace from the Grumman Gulfstream II, Gulfstream IIIs and IVs have been adopted by the Armed Forces as VIP aircraft. The USAF currently operates 13 Gulfstream IIIs: three C-20As (83-0502 at Andrews AFB on 29 June 1990), seven C-20Bs, and three C-20Cs. It has ordered Gulfstream IVs as C-20Fs. (René J. Francillon)

The range of the Gulfstream III enables C-20s to operate far from their home base. This C-20B of the 89th MAW at Andrews AFB was photographed at Yokota AB, Japan, on 7 June 1991. (Toyokazu Matsuzaki)

Departing with the Secretary of the Air Force, Dr. Sheila E. Widnall, from Rodeo '94, C-20C (86-0204) was photographed at McChord AFB in June 1994. (Jim Dunn)

In February 1994, a total of 83 C-21As were in Air Force service. Four were with the Air National Guard, six with PACAF, six with Air Force Space Command, seven with Air Force Materiel Command (including 84-0118 of the 375th AW photographed at Nellis AFB on 23 June 1992), 10 with Air Education and Training Command, 12 with USAFE, 13 with Air Combat Command, and 25 with Air Mobility Command. (René J. Francillon)

Bearing the tail code CS of the 21st Space Wing at Peterson AFB, Colorado, 84-0106 was photographed at Beale AFB, California, in May 1994. (Jim Dunn)

Contract personnel prepare to place wheel chokes as 84-0075, a C-21A assigned at Andrews AFB to the 457th Airlift Squadron, AMC, is parked under the tower at McChord AFB on 29 June 1994. (René J. Francillon)

Five 727 jetliners were acquired by the Air Force on the second-hand market. The C-22A (84-0193, built as a 727-030) is stored by the Aerospace Maintenance and Regeneration Center at Davis-Monthan AFB, Arizona, while the four C-22Bs remain in service with the Air National Guard. When this photograph was taken at Andrews AFB on 29 June 1990, the four C-22Bs were assigned to Det 1, HQ District of Columbia ANG. (René J. Francillon)

On 15 March 1992, Det 1, HQ District of Columbia ANG was elevated to squadron status as the 201st Airlift Squadron. Still assigned to the 113th Fighter Wing, the 201st AS is currently equipped with four C-21As and four C-22Bs. (Carl E. Porter)

83-4610, a C-22B of the 201st AS, DC ANG, caught just off runway 34 as it departs McChord AFB on 28 June 1994. (Jim Dunn)

The short-lived EDSA (European Distribution System Aircraft) program, which resulted in the acquisition of 18 C-23As, was initiated in 1982 to meet USAFE requirements for a low-cost logistic support aircraft to fly parts and components from warehouses at RAF Kemble, England, and Torrejon AB, Spain, to operational bases.

84-0463 in service with the 10th Military Airlift Squadron, USAFE, at Zweibrücken AB, Germany. The last C-23As departed Europe in November 1990, just six years after the ugliest aircraft ever to bear USAF markings had entered service.

When the C-23As were withdrawn from USAFE, three went to the Test Pilot School at Edwards AFB, seven went to the US Forestry Service for use as smoke-jumper transports, and eight went to the US Army as logistic support aircraft (including 84-0261 of the Corpus Christi Army Depot seen at Biggs Field, El Paso, on 20 April 1992). (René J. Francillon)

The 747 entered USAF service in December 1974 when the first of three E-4A Advanced Airborne Command Post aircraft was delivered. They were later brought up to E-4B standard to join 75-0175 (the first aircraft to be delivered to Bravo standard). All four E-4Bs are currently in service with the 1st ACCS, 55th Wing, at Offutt AFB, Nebraska. (Harrison W. Rued)

With the acquisition of two VC-25As, the Air Force joined the selected few who operate 747s in the VVIP transport role. Bills, including those for traffic delays at LAX, are footed by taxpayers not by friends of B & H. Other 747 VVIP operators are the sultanate of Brunei (one 747-400), the government of Japan (two 747-400s), the sultanate of Oman (one 747SP), and the kingdom of Saudi Arabia (one 747SP). (Jim Dunn)

Bringing President Clinton to California, Air Force One was photographed on 3 October 1993 as it was about to land on runway 16 at McClellan AFB. (Jim Dunn)

Main ANGOSTA for the ANG, the Fairchild-Swearingen C-26A was built in San Antonio, Texas. In Guard service, it has proven reliable but, unloved, has been nicknamed 'San Antonio sewer pipe' and 'San Antonio death tube.' This photo of the support aircraft of the 144th Wing, California ANG, may not convey the impression of death but certainly brings to the fore the tube-like appearance of the C-26. (René J. Francillon)

Designed, developed, and built in Italy by Alenia (previously Fiat and Aeritalia) the G222 was selected by the USAF as an austere STOL intratheater transport for assignment to the Southern Command. Fitted out to US standard by Chrysler Technologies Airborne Systems (CTAS), the aircraft is designated C-27A Spartan in USAF service. Bearing the HW tail code of the 24th Wing, 91-0105 was photographed at Howard AFB, Panama, in the spring of 1993. (Bill Curry)

To replace Lockheed C-140As used in the C-FIN (Combat Flight Inspection and Navigation) role, the Air Force ordered six specially-fitted British Aerospace 125 Srs 800As. Designated C-29As and delivered in 1989, these aircraft saw limited USAF service as the navaids checking mission was soon transferred to the Federal Aviation Administration. Shorn of their camouflage, the C-29As now serve with the FAA. (René J. Francillon)

The last operational units to fly C-130As were from the Tennessee ANG. The 105th Tactical Airlift Squadron in Nashville (to which belonged 56-0525 photographed at Pope AFB during Rodeo '89) converted to C-130Hs during FY90. The 155th TAS in Memphis converted to C-141Bs and was redesignated 155th AS in April 1992. (René J. Francillon)

Three squadrons equipped with C-130Bs were given the secondary mission of forest fire-fighting with two of their Herks being quickly fitted with MAFFS units when required. Belonging to the 187th TAS in Cheyenne, this aircraft drops water during a MAFFS training sortie in California. The Wyoming ANG squadron has now converted to C-130H but retains the MAFFS mission. (René J. Francillon)

After being withdrawn from tactical airlift squadrons, a number of older Herks were assigned to ANG units as operational support aircraft. Painted in air defense grey, as befits its assignment to the 142d Fighter Interceptor Group, Oregon ANG, this C-130B is seen landing at the Portland IAP in October 1989. (Carl E. Porter)

As this C-130E photographed at Pope AFB in June 1992 carries prominent tiger mouth markings, no prize will be awarded for identifying it as an aircraft of the 23d Wing of Flying Tigers fame. (Jim Dunn)

Carrying appropriate markings to celebrate the 40th anniversary of PACAF's Santa Claus mission – the air drop of gifts to isolated islanders in Micronesia – 63-7837, a C-130E of the 374th AW, prepares to depart Andersen AFB, Guam, on 16 December 1992. (Jim Dunn)

Back from the range, a pair of C-130Es of the 314th Airlift Wing at Little Rock AFB, Arkansas, taxies back to the transport ramp at Nellis AFB after flying a Red Flag mission in the morning of 16 February 1993. (René J. Francillon)

Competing in Rodeo '94, 63-7805, a C-130E of the 403d AW, AFRES, is lined up for a precision landing on the assault strip next to the main runway at McChord AFB. (René J. Francillon)

Flying low over the Santa Inez mountains, a C-130E crew from the 146th TAW at Channel Islands ANGB gains experience for its federal mission, tactical airlift, and for one of its state missions, forest fire-fighting. (René J. Francillon)

Now that they are AMC-gained, ANG C-130 units are adding tail codes. RI identifies the 143d AS, 143d AG, of the Rhode Island ANG at the Quonset State Airport. (René J. Francillon)

Based at Elmendord AFB, Alaska, PACAF's 3d Wing is comprised of two squadrons of F-15C/Ds (19th FS and 54th FS), the 90th FS with F-15Es, the 962d AWACS with E-3Bs, and the 517th AS with C-130Hs (including 74-2062 photographed at McChord AFB on 29 June 1994) and C-12Fs. (René J. Francillon)

Texans do it in the dirt: A C-130H of the 181st TAS, 136th TAW, Texas ANG, makes an assault landing at the Sicily strip, Ft Bragg, North Carolina, in June 1990. (Jim Dunn)

83-0491, one of four ski-equipped LC-130Hs of the 139th AS, 109th AG. Based in Schenectady, this New York ANG unit is tasked with arctic and antarctic resupply. (Jim Dunn)

Soon to be replaced by AC-130Hs as the active duty 16th SOS at Hurlburt Field converts to AC-130Us, AC-130As of the 711th SOS, 919th SOW, AFRES, have amply earned the right to be retired. By the end of February 1994, the low-time AC-130A had been flown 13,279 hours while the high-time aircraft had logged 18,922 hours. (Jim Dunn)

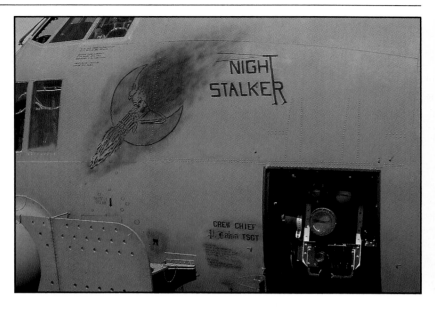

The AC-130Hs which the reservists will inherit from the 16th SOS will not be much younger as by the end of February 1994 they had logged between 12,020 and 13,987 hours. However, the AC-130H weapons systems represent a significant upgrade over those of the AC-130As. (USAF)

A few cans of paint can do wonders for old girls. First serving as a tactical airlifter with 61st TAS, 69-6569 was soon modified to AC-130H. She looks surprisingly young in her grey coat. (Paul Minert)

By the end of January 1994, 69-6572 had logged 12,938 flight hours. Port side front view of this AC-130H provides detail of AN/ASD-5 'Black Crow' ignition sensor installation beneath the cockpit, 20-mm M61 A1 cannon on forward fuselage side, and AN/AAD-7 infrared sensor mounted forward on main gear fairing. Aft of the main gear housing can be seen barrels of 40-mm Bofors cannon and 105-mm howitzer and radome housing AN/APQ-150 beacon tracking radar. (Carl E. Porter)

SUU-42A/A chaff dispensing pod and AN/ALQ-187 ECM pod tandem installation beneath port wing of AC-130H. (Carl E. Porter)

The data block next to the cockpit of this Herk photographed in October 1991 at Edwards AFB says 'C-130U-365-LM.' In fact, aircraft 87-0128 is the first AC-130U obtained by modifying a brand new C-130H-365-LM. (Jim Dunn)

63-7869, an EC-130E of the 193rd SOS, in the initial Rivet Rider configuration. Based at Harrisburg, this Pennsylvania ANG unit obtained its first Rivet Rider airborne radio/television station in August 1977. (René J. Francillon)

Upgraded to gain color TV broadcast capability, EC-135Es in the new Rivet Rider configuration have four distinctive tail-mounted antennas, and a large underwing equipment pot outboard of the axe-blade antenna beneath both outboard wing panels. 63-7773 was photographed in October 1994 at the Harrisburg IAP where Pennsylvania ANG's 193d SOS is based. (Michael L. Grove)

Senior Scout EC-130Es are quickly configured for their classified electronic warfare mission. Equipment and operators are enclosed in special air-conditioned containers. Aerials are attached to panels replacing standard parachute doors and main gear doors as well as under the tail. Belonging to the 193d SOS, Pennsylvania ANG, 63-7816 was photographed during Green Flag in April 1994. (Jim Dunn)

The end of an era. In January 1988, the Air Force still carried 32 piston-engined C-131s in its inventory. Two C-131Bs, eight C-131Ds, and two C-131Es were used as state headquarters transports by the ANG, while eight C-131Bs, 10 C-131Ds (including 54-2820 which had last been assigned to the Washington ANG), and two C-131Es were in storage at Davis-Monthan AFB. In addition, the turboprop-powered NC-131H was bailed to Calspan for use as a variable stability testbed. (Jim Dunn)

54-5822, the much regretted C-131D of the California ANG, was replaced by a Fairchild C-26A in July 1989. On 28 February 1994, two C-131Bs remained in storage while the NC-131H was still with Calspan. (René J. Francillon)

Photographed at Gowen Field, Boise, on 16 July 1988, the C-131D of the Idaho ANG was undergoing an engine change. When it was retired, 55-0300 had logged nearly 16,000 hours and was in the superb condition usually associated with Guard-maintained aircraft. (Christian Jacquet)

60-0378, one of the last two C-135As in USAF service, shows off its spit shine as it lands at Nellis AFB on 18 September 1991. Last operated by the 55th Wing at Offutt AFB, Nebraska, it was withdrawn from use in 1993. (René J. Francillon)

Photographed at Yokota AB, Japan, on 14 May 1991, this C-135C (61-2668) was then assigned to Det 1, 89th MAW. (Toyokazu Matsuzaki)

Still wearing the distinctive paint scheme of the 89th MAW, the presidential and VIP wing at Andrews AFB, 61-2668 is now assigned to the 15th Air Base Wing at Hickam AFB, Hawaii. (Carl E. Porter)

The end of the Cold War is accelerating the phase-out of EC-135s. There were 48 in service in January 1988, but only 17 remained in February 1994. After logging slightly less than 12,000 hours, this EC-135A was transferred to the Offutt AFB Museum in February 1992. The tail code OF was never carried when 61-0287 was in service. (Douglas D. Olson)

After being reengined with TF33 turbofans, four EC-135Ns were redesignated EC-135Es. Having logged 17,131 hours by 28 February 1994, 61-0326 was still operated by the 4950th Test Wing at Wright-Patterson AFB, Ohio. (René J. Francillon)

Carrying the tail markings of the 4th ACCS, 28th Bomb Wing, based at Ellsworth AFB, South Dakota, 62-3579 was photographed on approach to Mather AFB, California, on 14 April 1989. This EC-135G is now stored at Davis-Monthan AFB. (Jim Dunn)

Serving for most of its career with the 9th ACCS at Hickam AFB, Hawaii, this EC-135J was photographed on final to runway 32 at March AFB, California, on 1 May 1990. In 1992, 63-8055 was transferred to the 2d ACCS at Offutt AFB. In October 1993, by which time it had logged 13,993 hours, it was flown to Davis-Monthan AFB for storage at AMARC. (René J. Francillon)

The use of C-135/KC-135 airframes with their cargo loading door on the forward fuselage facilitated installation of large equipment consoles in EC-135s and RC-135s. Equipment fit, however, was often tight as shown by this photo of an EC-135J. (Carl E. Porter)

Two EC-135K command & control aircraft are still operated by the 8th Tactical Deployment Control Squadron at Tinker AFB. 55-3118 was photographed at this Oklahoma base on 1 May 1989. (René J. Francillon)

KC-135As were first assigned to the 93d Air Refueling Squadron at Castle AFB, California, on 18 January 1957 and served with that squadron for 37 years. 63-8887 was photographed at the Sacramento Metro Airport during instrument landing training on 10 March 1988. One of many cosmetic changes which the Air Force of the nineties seems to favor has seen AREFS, AREFG, and AREFW abbreviations replaced by ARS, ARG, and ARG. Pray tell why. (Jim Dunn)

57-1432, a KC-135A of the 43d AREFS photographed at Fairchild AFB, Washington, on 15 July 1988. Since reengined to KC-135R standard, this aircraft was with the 380th ARW at Plattsburgh AFB, New York, in February 1994. (Christian Jacquet)

On 28 February 1994, the Air Force was left with only 11 operational KC-135As, six assigned to Castle AFB, three to Dyess AFB, and two to Barksdale AFB. Sixty others, including 56-3601 seen here on approach to Castle AFB on 2 November 1992, were stored. Stored aircraft are starting to be sold to allies for conversion to KC-135R standard (five to France and ten to Turkey). (René J. Francillon)

For the AFRES and the ANG, reengining KC-135As with JT3D turbofans purchased from airlines proved an economical way of improving Stratotanker performance and reliability while reducing noise complaints. For units based at bases subject to prolonged freezing temperatures, such as the Salt Lake City IAP and Hill AFB where the Utah ANG kept tankers on alert, dispensing with the water injection system of the KC-135As greatly eased winter operations. (Jim Dunn)

For pilots of the 146th TFS at the Greater Pittsburgh IAP, converting from A-7Ds to KC-135Es was a bitter experience. 56-3612 was photographed at McClellan AFB, California, on 22 April 1993, 18 months after this Pennsylvania ANG unit had been redesignated 146th ARS. (René J. Francillon)

Rodeo '94, McChord AFB, June 1994: The grey KC-135E entered by the 452d Air Mobility Wing, AFRES, parked in front of green KC-135Rs representing the 19th and 22d Air Refueling Wings. (René J. Francillon)

To support SR-71 operations near Siberia, China, and North Korea, KC-135Qs were based at Kadena AB. Bearing markings of the 909th AREFS, 376th Strategic Wing, 58-0069 was photographed at the Okinawa base on 4 September 1988. (Robert S. Hopkins III)

The main gear is starting to retract as 58-0129 climbs away on 20 April 1990. SR-71s had been withdrawn less than three months earlier but the 9th SRW at Beale AFB then still had two KC-135Q squadrons, the 349th and the 350th. (René J. Francillon)

By the time BB tail codes were applied to KC-135Qs of the 9th Wing, the 349th ARS had been inactivated. Remaining at Beale AFB, the 350th ARS was briefly transferred from Air Combat Command to Air Mobility Command before being inactivated. (Jim Dunn)

Fitted with flexible hose-and-basket at the end of its refueling boom, a KC-135R of the 19th ARW prepares to transfer fuel to probe-equipped naval aircraft during a Desert Storm strike on 22 January 1991. (Rick Morgan)

Underside view of 62-3540, a KC-135R of the 29th Bomb Wing, SAC, emphasizes the large size of the F108-CF-100 nacelles. (Jim Dunn)

'Lone Wolf,' a KC-135R of the 340th AREFW at Altus AFB on 2 May 1989. Tankers from this unit generally wore nose art reflecting the Indian heritage of the Sooner State. (René J. Francillon)

Soaking in the late afternoon sun, 58-0106 of the 93d Wing is about to land on runway 31 at Castle AFB on 2 November 1992. Official closure date for this California base is 30 September 1995. (René J. Francillon)

Having had to rely for too long on SAC tankers deployed TDY with the European Tanker Task Force at RAF Mildenhall and RAF Fairford, USAFE gained its own KC-135 unit with the activation of the 100th Air Refueling Wing at RAF Mildenhall in January 1992. Fin markings for its KC-135Rs have a definite 'Brit' allure in keeping with the basing of this unit in Suffolk. (Christian Jacquet)

Two squadrons of the 121st ARW, Ohio ANG, are equipped with KC-135Rs. Bearing the blue fin band of the 166th ARS, 57-1469 turns onto runway 34 at McChord AFB to take-off for a Rodeo '94 sortie. (René J. Francillon)

64-14847, an RC-135U of the 55th SRW, at Offutt AFB, Nebraska on 19 July 1991. Towel-rail antenna have now been removed from above the cheek fairing on both sides of forward fuselage. (Robert S. Hopkins III)

Photographed at Mather AFB on 18 June 1988, this RC-135V had brought the 55th SRW commander to this California base to attend a commanders' conference. (Peter B. Lewis)

Always discrete during their SAC days, RC-135s and EC-135s assigned to the 55th Wing gained OF tail code following the activation of Air Combat Command. 64-14842, an RC-135V, lands at Nellis AFB in April 1994 at the end of a Green Flag sortie. (Jim Dunn)

As the 'Ears of the Storm,' RC-135s played a discrete but vital role during Desert Storm. Beginning at the onset of Desert Shield and continuing well past the cease fire, Rivet Joint crews and aircraft rotated between Offutt AFB and their operating base in Riyadh. (Peter B. Lewis)

Photographed on 18 September 1991, this RC-135W (62-4135) carries on its fuselage the Milky Way stripe as Strategic Air Command was not disbanded until nearly nine months later. A few days after this photograph was taken the 55th SRW was redesignated 55th Wing. (René J. Francillon)

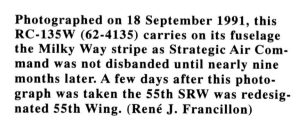

'Hog' nose and cheek fairings of the TC-135W do not house sensors and are fitted for aerodynamic purpose, thus providing this pilot trainer version with handling characteristics similar to those of operational Rivet Joint aircraft. 62-4129 was photographed at Beale AFB on 27 October 1991. (Jim Dunn)

61-2665, a WC-135B of the 55th Weather Reconnaissance Squadron at McClellan AFB, California, returns to its base on 18 November 1988. The camera port in the upper deck cargo loading door was retrofitted for the Star Cast electro-optical system. (Jim Dunn)

Returning to the 55th WRS ramp at McClellan AFB, 61-2666 taxies below the tower on 20 May 1991. Having logged 25,168 hours by 28 February 1994, this aircraft was then at Wright-Patterson AFB to be fitted with specialized equipment and accommodation for use as an OC-135B Open Skies platform. (Jim Dunn)

Ten C-135Bs were converted by Hayes International as WC-135B weather reconnaissance aircraft but later conversion resulted in several redesignations. On 28 February 1994, three WC-135Bs, one TC-135B pilot trainer, and one OC-135B Open Skies platform (61-2674 photographed on 7 September 1994) were operated by the 55th Wing at Offutt AFB. Two other WC-135Bs were being modified as OC-135Bs, one was a C-135C staff transport assigned to the 15th Air Base Wing, and another C-135C was with the 412th Test Wing. (Harrison W. Rued)

VIP tails at Andrews AFB on 29 June 1990. 62-4126, a C-135B, is now used as a pilot trainer by the 108th ARW, New Jersey ANG, at McGuire AFB. 85-6973, a C-137C, was still with the 89th Airlift Wing in February 1994. (René J. Francillon)

58-6972 was the third and last J57-powered aircraft delivered as a VC-137As for the Special Air Mission. Reengined with TF33 turbofans, it was redesignated C-137B (the definitely non-PC V prefix being dropped). In February 1994, it remained with the 89th Airlift Wing at Andrews AFB. (René J. Francillon)

The first aircraft to carry the C-137C designation (initially VC-137C) were ordered new as Air Force One (62-6000) and its back-up (72-7000). Two ex-airline 707s acquired in 1985 were also given the C-137C designation (including 85-6974 photographed on approach to McClellan AFB on 19 April 1990). Reflecting the higher level of utilization achieved by commercial operators, the two ex-airline C-137Cs had logged 44,975 and 51,113 hours by the end of February 1994 whereas the two original Air Force aircraft had flown only 10,935 and 5,800 hours. (Jim Dunn)

Winner of the 1956 UCX (utility cargo) competition, the four-engined Lockheed JetStar was ordered by the Air Force for navaids checking with MATS Airway and Air Communications Service (five C-140As including this aircraft photographed in April 1988) and for staff/VIP transports (five C-140Bs and six VC-140Bs). (Carl E. Porter)

Six VC-140Bs (61-2488/61-2493) were acquired for the 1254th Air Transport Wing (Special Mission). The Andrews AFB unit was redesignated 89th Military Airlift Wing (Special Mission) on 8 January 1966. By January 1988, its VC-140Bs had been withdrawn from use. (Peter B. Lewis)

By January 1988, only one of five C-140Bs remained in service (62-4201 assigned to the 58th MAS at Ramstein AB, Germany). 62-4197, seen here on 19 November 1991, was stored at AMARC after logging 13,645 hours in USAF service. (Carl E. Porter)

65-0239, a C-141B of the 60th MAW, banks sharply to reach the runway while practicing combat approaches at Travis AFB in October 1989. (Carl E. Porter)

The 60th Military Airlift Wing at Travis AFB provided much logistic support during the war in Southeast Asia. However, in the mind of many, the wing's association with the Vietnam War is more easily remembered for happy memories of Operation Homecoming, the return of POWs released by North Vietnam, and for its sadder duty of bringing home the remains of KIAs and MIAs. Sadly, that grim task is ongoing. In spite of our selfish pursuit of happiness, we ought never to forget their supreme sacrifice. (Carl E. Porter)

The need to support Desert Shield and Desert Storm placed a tremendous load on Military Airlift Command. Time was not always available to repaint aircraft out of PDM as shown by this C-141B (65-9411 of the 438th MAW, AFRES, at McGuire AFB, New Jersey) flying into Hickam AFB in plain natural finish. (Carl E. Porter)

When Arab forces launched their surprise attack against Israel on Yom Kippur 1973, the Air Force was tasked to fly urgently needed ammunition and parts to the Middle East. Heavily depending on Arab oil, our European allies were unwilling to grant landing rights to USAF aircraft operating in support of the Jewish State, thus convincing the Air Force of the need of fitting an aerial refueling receptacle to C-141As being stretched into C-141Bs. (Carl E. Porter)

C-141B of the 60th MAW about to touch down on runway 21R at Travis AFB. (Carl E. Porter)

Even though its 437th MAW crew nicknamed it '4 Sick 18,' aircraft 0618 (C-141B, 64-0618) won the preflight competition during Rodeo '89 at Pope AFB in June 1989. That earned it a near record number of 'zaps.' (René J. Francillon)

Carrying the red fin band identifying the 964th AWACS, E-3B (76-1605) returns to Nellis AFB at the end of a Red Flag sortie on 19 April 1990. (René J. Francillon)

Sun and stormy skies highlight 82-0006, an E-3C from the 965th AWACS (yellow fin band), about to land at Nellis AFB in July 1990. (René J. Francillon)

Dumping fuel as take-off weight is close to exceeding limits on a hot late spring day at Nellis AFB, an E-3B (71-1408) of the 965th AWACS departs Nellis AFB on 4 June 1991. (Jim Dunn)

Carrying the yellow fin band of the 965th AWACS, this Sentry (77-0355) was delivered in E-3A configuration but had been upgraded to E-3B standard by the time it was photographed on approach to Nellis AFB on 19 September 1991. (René J. Francillon)

E-3B (76-1607) of the 963d AWACS at Nellis AFB on 5 June 1991. Noteworthy are the Have Siren IR jammer mounted on the trailing edge of the engine pylons. (René J. Francillon)

The switch from TAC to ACC brought about the addition of tail codes. 79-0003, an OK-coded E-3B from the 963d AWACS, returns to Nellis AFB at the end of a Green Flag sortie in April 1994. (Jim Dunn)

Being an ex-QANTAS 707-338C, this E-8A was appropriately photographed in March 1989 at the Melbourne Airport, not that in Australia but the Florida home of the prime contractor for the Joint STARS. (Robert E. Kling)

Even though acceptance trials had not yet been completed, the two E-8A prototypes were rushed to Saudi Arabia and proved of great value during Desert Storm. (Robert E. Kling)

Two civil-registered de Havilland Canada E-9As are operated by the 475th Weapons Evaluation Group at Tyndall AFB, Florida, as missile range control aircraft. (Gary Chambers)

Flying between two cloud layers late in the afternoon of 14 July 1988, F-4C 63-7557, one of the last F-4Cs of the 123d FIS, catches the last rays of the sun off the coast of Oregon. (René J. Francillon)

The second production F-4C, 63-7407 had only logged 2,768 hours when it was phased out of service at the Air Force Flight Test Center. (Jim Dunn)

Last assigned to the 171st FIS, Michigan ANG, this F-4C became a battle damage training aircraft with the 51st Wing at Osan AB after being withdrawn from operations. No longer airworthy, it was photographed at the Korean base in August 1991. (Bill Curry)

With immaculate paint scheme and a full load of Sparrows and Sidewinders, the boss' bird from the 924th TFG, the AFRES unit at Bergstrom AFB, Texas, plays centerfold in August 1988. Early during the following year, the 924th converted from F-4Ds to F-4Es. For the 'Outlaws,' the Phantom era ended in 1991 with their conversion to F-16A/Bs. (Carl E. Porter)

While his wingman is at the boom, this F-4D from the AFRES squadron at Wright-Patterson AFB, the 89th TFS, awaits its turn below and behind the tanker's port wing. (René J. Francillon)

The sight and sound of an F-4 taxiing with drag chute billowing in the J79 exhausts are very much missed by enthusiasts. The 144th FIW, the Fresno-based ANG unit to which belonged this F-4D, completed its conversion to F-16 ADF in October 1989. (Carl E. Porter)

The sixth production F-4E, 66-0289, logged virtually most of its 4,800 flight hours at Edwards AFB. Never brought up to full production standard, it was eventually designated NF-4E to reflect its permanent assignment to test status. (Carl E. Porter)

The last F-4E assigned to the 110th TFS, Missouri ANG, left St Louis in September 1991. Bomb racks empty, 68-0345 returns from an air support training sortie at the National Training Center, Ft Irwin, California. (Carl E. Porter)

F-4E-40-MC of the 108th TFS at McGuire AFB on 23 June 1990. When this New Jersey ANG unit converted to tankers, most of its F-4Es went to the Republic of Korea Air Force and the Turkish Air Force. Its last F-4E was flown out on 7 October 1991. (René J. Francillon)

F-4E-61-MC of the 21st Tactical Fighter Training Squadron on 3 June 1991 at George AFB. This California base closed in December 1992. Perhaps paying for the fact that many of its representatives have, at best, been lukewarm in their support of the military, Californians have been particularly hard hit by base closures. Gone are Castle, George, Hamilton, Mather, and Norton AFBs while March AFB is to be downgraded to reserve status, the future of McClellan AFB is in doubt, and the number of aircraft assigned to Beale AFB has markedly decreased. (René J. Francillon)

Still carrying the tail code PN denoting that it had last been assigned to the 3d TFW at Clark AB, The Philippines, 73-1204 is a F-4E-59-MC modified to QF-4E standard by Tracor-Flight Systems Inc. Photographed at Mojave on 6 June 1992, this aircraft was still there on 28 February 1994. (Jim Dunn)

The last F-4E squadron, the 20th FS, provides F-4 training for the Deutsche Luftwaffe. It was transferred from the 35th FW at George AFB (with code GA) to the 49th FW at Holloman AFB (with code HO) just before the California base closed. (Paul Negri)

The first two F-4Gs assigned to USAFE arrived at Spangdahlem AB on 28 March 1979 and the 81st TFS, 52d TFW, completed its conversion from Wild Weasel F-4Cs to F-4Gs on 26 July 1979. USAFE last four F-4Gs left their German base on 18 February 1994. (René J. Francillon)

Carrying the tail code OT of the Tactical Air Warfare Center at Eglin AFB, this F-4G (69-7235) from Det 5, 4485th Test Squadron, was photographed at George AFB on 3 June 1991. Earlier, this detachment had carried the tail code WW. (René J. Francillon)

Before Desert Storm, the Air Force had decided to phase out F-4Gs from active duty units. Combat operations against Iraq drove home the necessity of retaining specialized SEAD aircraft as firing HARMs without AN/APR-47 and a second crew member did not turn single-seat F-16Cs into effective Wild Weasels. Accordingly, a new Wild Weasel squadron, the 561st FS, was activated at Nellis AFB on 1 February 1993. (Jim Dunn)

Before reversing course and activating the 561st FS, the Air Force had planned to assign the Wild Weasel mission to two RF-4C guard units, those in Idaho and Nevada. Among the aircraft received by the 124th FG at Gowen Field, Boise, were many veterans of Desert Storm. The cover over the forward right side antenna of its AN/APR-47 proudly advertises that 69-7263 had served during the Gulf War. (René J. Francillon)

F-4Gs returned to southwest Asia in March 1993 when the Idaho ANG sent a first Wild Weasel detachment on TDY to Saudi Arabia to replace the USAFE F-4G detachment previously assigned to the 4404th Composite Wing at Dhahran RSAFB. 69-7261 was photographed in Saudi Arabia in early 1994. (N. Donald)

Flight level 210, 315 KIAS, 7 June 1994, 1515Z: 'Custer 1' flies over northern Nevada, near Winnemuca. Note that this F-4G (69-7263) of the 124th Fighter Group, Idaho ANG, has been fitted with a one piece windshield. (René J. Francillon)

In January 1988, 161 RF-4Cs were assigned to active duty reconnaissance squadrons. Twenty-three were with USAFE, 23 with PACAF, and 115 with TAC. Of the latter, 25 (including 67-0464) were with the 16th TRS, 363d TFW, at Shaw AFB, South Carolina. (Peter B. Lewis)

Representing USAFE at the 1988 Reconnaissance Air Meet (RAM '88), this RF-4C of the 38th TRS, 26th TRW, awaits brake release at Bergstrom AFB. Squadron and wing were inactivated during the first week in April 1991. (Carl E. Porter)

The last active duty squadron to fly the RF-4C in its intended role was the 12th TRS, 67th TRW, at Bergstrom AFB, Texas. Bearing the Blackbirds tail fin cap of this squadron, 72-0149 was photographed at the end of a Red Flag sortie on 19 September 1991. (René J. Francillon)

Flown to Bahrein during Desert Shield by its owner, the 106th TRS of the Alabama ANG, 64-1047 was flown by crews from the 192d TRS of the Nevada ANG during Desert Storm. It was photographed in Reno on 11 April 1991, a couple days after it had been flown back from the Gulf. (René J. Francillon)

Prior to and during the Gulf War, RF-4Cs, the 'Eyes of the Storm,' were based at Sheikh Isa AB in Bahrein. The nose art on 65-0893 proclaims proudly that the 152d TRG, Nevada ANG, flew 412 sorties. This represented an average of 1.6 daily sorties per aircraft during the six-week war. (René J. Francillon)

The 173d Reconnaissance Squadron made its final appearance at Red Flag in February 1993. The Nebraska ANG then converted to KC-135Rs and its flying squadron became the 173d ARS. (René J. Francillon)

The Air National Guard, which received its first RF-4C in February 1971, has a long and very successful association with the recce Phantom. The ANG had 153 RF-4Cs with six squadrons in January 1988. Five years later there still were 92 RF-4Cs with five squadrons, but by February 1994 only 46 RF-4Cs remained, 29 with the Nevada Guard and 17 with the Alabama ANG. The latter had by then been notified that its Birmingham unit was to convert to tankers. (Jim Dunn)

Last Guard unit to convert to RF-4Cs, the 196th TRS flew recce Phantoms for only three years beginning during the spring of 1990. This pair of Grizzlies was photographed on 18 May 1993, days before this California ANG units sent its RF-4Cs to the boneyard. (René J. Francillon)

66-0408 of the 192d RS, 192d RG, over New Mexico, near Tucumcari, on 17 June 1994. Last Air Force unit to fly RF-4Cs, the Nevada ANG hopes to be re-equipped with recce-configured F-16Cs. Delays with that program may result in a less attractive conversion. (René J. Francillon)

Nose up, 74-1578 is about to touch down on runway 3 Left at Nellis AFB after tangling with French Jaguars over the Nevada range. The first aggressor squadron at Nellis AFB, the 64th Fighter Weapons Squadron (Aggressors), was activated on 15 October 1972 and was followed in July 1975 by the 65th. In April 1989, the 65th Aggressor Squadron inactivated and the 64th completed its conversion from F-5E/Fs to F-16C/Ds. (René J. Francillon)

With Soviet-style blue 46 and blue 30 on their nose, 73-0846 and 73-1530 caught at brakes release at the start of a Red Flag sortie. (René J. Francillon)

Wrap around camouflage proved highly effective during ACM over the range. Unlike most other aircraft retired from USAF service which are sent to AMARC to bake in the Arizona sun before ending up with a smelter, F-5s were quickly disposed of. Some went to the Navy, primarily with VFA-127 at NAS Fallon, others went to VMFT-401 at MCAS Yuma, and the remainders were supplied to Brazil and Honduras. (René J. Francillon)

Flying the F-5 with one of the aggressor squadrons was great even though one occasionally had to indulge the whims of press photographers. Captain Scott 'Patio' Patillo was indeed remarkably patient on the ground and appeared to have left all his aggressiveness on the range. (René J. Francillon)

83-0074 of one of the two aggressor squadrons at Nellis AFB. Noteworthy in this side profile is the extended nosewheel leg and the fully open louvered auxiliary doors on the aft fuselage. (René J. Francillon)

83-0073, seen here taxiing between runway 3 Left and 3 Right at Nellis AFB before taking off for the range is one of three ex-USAF F-5Fs which went to the Força Aérea Brasileira (Brazilian Air Force) in 1989. (René J. Francillon)

The 425th TFTS at Williams AFB mainly provided F-5 training for foreign pilots but also trained pilots for the US aggressor squadrons. 71-1400 is on final to runway 30 Center at this Arizona training base. Centerline tank and empty wingtip missile rails was a typical configuration for initial training sorties. (René J. Francillon)

73-1401 departing for a training sortie at Williams AFB. In 1989, after the 425th TFTS had ceased F-5 operations, this aircraft became one of 14 F-5Es transferred to Brazil. (René J. Francillon)

The last USAF F-5 squadron, the 425th Tactical Fighter Training Squadron, flew its final sortie on 31 August 1989. The following day, it was inactivated at Williams AFB. (René J. Francillon)

Afterburners aglow, a F-15A of the 122d TFS blasts off the runway at NAS New Orleans. After converting from F-4Cs to early production F-15A/Bs, the Louisiana ANG used colored tail bands and eagle scrolls with pilot and crew chief names beneath the cockpit to identify flights, 73-0090 being assigned to Red Flight. (Jim Dunn)

Lots of wing and lots of power, as shown by this LY-coded F-15A, account for most of the Eagle's superb combat capability. The facts that its radar and missiles are reliable and its pilots well trained were also factors to which Saddam Hussein ought to have paid more attention. (René J. Francillon)

The cockpit of the F-15, as illustrated by that of an aircraft from the 123d FS, Oregon ANG, endows Eagle pilots with superb visibility in almost every direction. (René J. Francillon)

Returning from a check flight after undergoing PDM at the Sacramento Air Logistics Center in April 1991, this F-15A stripped of paint displays a spurious serial on its starboard rudder: there was no 77-0022 Eagle. The aircraft is likely to have been 75-0122, a F-15A-13-MC. (Peter B. Lewis)

F-15A-19-MC of the 7th TFS, 49th TFW, landing at Nellis AFB on 5 June 1991. The 49th TFW at Holloman AFB, New Mexico, converted from F-4Ds to F-15A/Bs in 1977 and won top honors at William Tell '88. The 49th no longer flies F-15s and in 1994 was comprised of three F-117 squadrons, an HH-60G squadron, an AT-38B squadron providing training for the ROKAF, and two squadrons providing training for the Luftwaffe (one with F-4Es and one with German Tornadoes). (René J. Francillon)

Defenders of paradise. The 199th TFS (199th FS after March 1992), Hawaii ANG, gained sole responsibility for the defense of Hawaii in March 1969. It converted from F-4Cs to F-15A/Bs in 1987-88. (Carl E. Porter)

The 405th TTW at Luke AFB was the primary F-15 training unit. At peak strength in 1988, the wing was comprised of a F-5 squadron, the 425th TFTS based at nearby Williams AFB to take advantage of Northrop's support to T-38 operations at this ATC base, and of four F-15 squadrons, the 426th, 461st, 550th (in the markings of which F-15B 76-0129 is illustrated), and 555th Tactical Fighter Training Squadrons. (Christian Jacquet)

Undergoing post-PDM test, this unpainted F-15B-19-MC returns to McClellan AFB in April 1992. At the end of February 1994, having logged 4,304 hours, 77-0157 was with the AETC's 325 FW at Tyndall AFB, Florida. (Jim Dunn)

Photographed in April 1994, this F-15B-9-MC of the 39th Test Squadron, 46th Test Wing, carries the tail code OT of the Air Force Development Test Center at Eglin AFB, Florida. (Jim Dunn)

For a relatively short period in the late eighties, a few F-15s were finished in a darker grey scheme as illustrated by 82-0028 of the 57th Fighter Weapons Wing landing at Nellis AFB. (René J. Francillon)

Operating from Iceland, where diversionary fields are distant, F-15Cs of the 57th FIS usually carry CFTs (conformal fuel tanks), as illustrated by 80-0027 photographed at Nellis AFB on 15 March 1990. The squadron, now designated 57th FS, is one of two flying units currently assigned to the 35th Wing at NAS Keflavik. (René J. Francillon)

In March 1990, when 85-0112 of the 58th TFS was photographed at Nellis AFB carrying AIM-120 training rounds, the 33d TFW had begun qualifying with AMRAAMs. However, the new BVR missiles were not operationally ready when the 58th TFS deployed to Tabuk, Saudi Arabia, and 16 of its 17 kills were obtained with older AIM-7s. Another Iraqi aircraft was maneuvered into the ground. (René J. Francillon)

Led by 87-0001, the flagship of the 53d TFS, a foursome of Bitburg Eagles lines up on the runway on 21 July 1992 (Jean Soenen)

Based at Kadena AB, the 18th Tactical Fighter Wing got into the Eagle business in September 1979 when the 67th TFS returned to Okinawa after converting from Wild Weasel F-4Cs to F-15C/Ds. Now also composed of three non-Eagle squadrons – the 33d RQS with HH-60Gs, the 909th ARS with KC-135Rs, and the 961st AWACS with E-3B/Cs – the 18th Wing retains three F-15C/D squadrons, the 12th, 44th, and 67th Fighter Squadrons. (Carl E. Porter)

The Air Force does not have the PR of the Navy (such as the Top Gun movie) and McDonnell Douglas may not go to as much trouble to demonstrate the capability of the Eagle as Sukhoi goes to show off the Flanker, but the F-15/USAF fighter pilot training combination remains without equal. (René J. Francillon)

A pair of F-15Ds (88-0044 and 88-0048) of the Tactical Fighter Weapons Center at Nellis AFB on 5 June 1991. TFWC was redesignated USAF Fighter Weapons Center on 1 November 1991 and USAF Weapons and Tactics Center on 5 June 1992. (René J. Francillon)

F-15D-23-MC of the 95th FS, 325th FW, at Tyndall AFB, Florida, photographed on 24 June 1992 during a deployment to the USAF Weapons and Tactics Center at Nellis AFB. (René J. Francillon)

Two squadrons of the 3d Wing at Elmendorf AFB, Alaska, currently fly F-15C/Ds. Eagles of the 54th FS (including 79-0009 photographed at Klamath Falls, Oregon, during Sentry Eagle '93) have a yellow band on the outboard side of their fins, those of the 19th FS have a blue band in the same location. (Carl E. Porter)

Whether it be called Strike Eagle or, more familiarly Beagle (Bomber Eagle), the F-15E is a potent strike aircraft retaining most of the capability of the F-15 fighter versions and adding precise attack capability at low level and in adverse weather. The 57th Fighter Weapons Wing at Nellis AFB received its first five F-15Es in October 1989. (René J. Francillon)

F-15E training has taken place at Luke AFB since the summer of 1987. The 550th TFTS (in the markings of which 87-0177 was photographed at Travis AFB, California, in October 1993) was the second squadron of the 405th Tactical Training Wing to convert to LA-coded F-15Es. Following its transfer to the 58th Fighter Wing, the 461st and 550th Fighter Squadrons have flown LF-coded F-15Es. (Carl E. Porter)

Gunsmoke '93 at Nellis AFB in October 1993: a F-15E from the 90th FS, 3d Wing, PACAF, returns from the range. (Jim Dunn)

Three years after the Gulf War, the Air Force still has to be prepared to counter foolish moves by Saddam Hussein. Loaded with GBU-12 Paveway II laser-guided bombs and carrying AIM-120As and AIM-9Ls for self-defense, 88-1675, a F-15E-45-MC of the 4th Wing stands ready at Dhahran, Saudi Arabia. (N. Donald)

Carrying six Mk 82 bombs, a light load for the Strike Eagle, a F-15E-47-MC of the 335th FS has no problem climbing away in full burners. (Jim Dunn)

In the spring of 1994, the aircraft of the commander of the 391st FS, 366th Wing, carried the name Gen. Merrill A. McPeak (then USAF Chief of Staff) under its cockpit on the port side. 87-0210 is seen here taxiing at McChord AFB, Washington, on 27 June 1994 (René J. Francillon)

F-16A-15K-CF of the 421st TFS, 388th TFW, at Hill AFB on 20 July 1988. The 388th began converting from F-16A/Bs to F-16C/D Block 40 aircraft in May 1989. (René J. Francillon)

78-0076 of the 466th TFS, 419th TFW. After this AFRES squadron at Hill AFB converted to F-16C/Ds, 78-0076 was transferred to the 89th FS at Wright-Patterson AFB, the reserve unit with which it was still serving in February 1994 after logging 2,979 hours. (René J. Francillon)

Ready to leave the DC ANG ramp at Andrews AFB, Maryland, on 29 June 1990, 80-0516 carries the tail code and fin markings of the 121st TFS, 113th TFW. (René J. Francillon)

The combined effects of steady F-16C production in the eighties and downsizing in the nineties have led the Air Force to accelerate F-16A phase-out from active duty units. In February 1994, there were only 18 F-16As left with active duty units, 95 were stored at Davis-Monthan AFB, and one was with Lockheed in Fort Worth. Photographed in May 1994, 78-0054 had just been transferred from the 46th Test Wing at Eglin AFB to the 412th Test Wing at Edwards AFB. (Jim Dunn)

In February 1994, the AFRES aircraft inventory still included 75 F-16As while 339 F-16As and F-16A ADFs were in the ANG inventory. With the possible exception of aircraft recently upgraded to ADF standard, these early Fighting Falcons (including 82-1017 from the 170th FS, Illinois ANG) will soon be replaced by F-16Cs made available by the downsizing of active duty components. (Carl E. Porter)

Delivered as a F-16A-05-CF to the 56th TTW at MacDill AFB, Florida, on 17 March 1980, 78-0058 was later included in the OCU (Operational Capability Upgrade) program. Shown in the markings of its current operator – the 107th FS, 127th FW, Michigan ANG – it had logged 3,502 hours by 28 February 1994. (Douglas D. Olson)

Carrying four live Mk 82 bombs, a F-16B of the 310th TFTS, 58th TTW, departs last chance at Luke AFB on its way to the Barry M. Goldwater Bombing and Gunnery Range south of Gila Bend, Arizona. (René J. Francillon)

78-0082, the sixth production F-16B, cleans up its gear on departure from Klamath Falls, Oregon, in August 1993. (Carl E. Porter)

F-16B-15H-CF of the 93d FS, 482d FW, AFRES photographed in October 1994 at Reno-Stead, Nevada. After Homestead AFB, Florida, was hard hit by Hurricane Andrews in August 1992, the 'Makos' had to relocate temporarily to Mac Dill AFB, Florida, while DOD decided whether or not to rebuild their base. Following a positive decision, Homestead is reopening as an Air Reserve Base. (Jim Dunn)

Major Jamie MacKay of the 144th FIW, California ANG, goes through his final check before taxiing his ADF out of the alert barn at George AFB on 14 March 1990. (René J. Francillon)

California air guardsmen upload an AIM-9P-3 on the missile rail beneath the port wing of a F-16A ADF from the 194th FIS, 144th FIW, at George AFB on 14 March 1990. (René J. Francillon)

Built as a F-16A-15J-CF and delivered on 24 June 1983 to the 474th TFW at Nellis AFB, 82-0913 was photographed at Klamath Falls on 13 July 1990. By then brought up to ADF standard, the aircraft carries tail markings of the 114th TFTS, Oregon ANG. (René J. Francillon)

Up to now, top honor for most attractive scheme applied to US F-16s goes to the 'Happy Hooligans' of Fargo, North Dakota, for the ADF assigned in 1989 to the commander of the 119th Fighter Interceptor Group. (Robert B. Greby)

Brought up to full ADF standard, this Fighting Falcon of the 171st FS was photographed at Selfridge ANGB in September 1992. Since then, this Michigan ANG squadron has converted to C-130Es and has been redesignated the 171st AS. (Douglas D. Olson)

'The Green Mountain Boys' of the Vermont ANG converted from F-4Ds to F-16As in 1986 and their Fighting Falcons were brought up to ADF standard during FY90. (Carl E. Porter)

F-16C Block 30 of the 23d TFS, 52d TFW, USAFE flying over solid overcast above Europe in May 1989. Currently the 23d FS is one of four fighter squadrons assigned to Spangdahlem AB, Germany. The others are the 22d also flying F-16C/Ds, the 53d FS with F-15C/Ds, and the 81st with A/OA-10As. (Armée de l'air)

84-1247, a F-16C Block 25 of the 17th TFS, 363d TFW, takes off from Nellis AFB on 18 September 1991 carrying an AN/ALQ-119(V)-15 ECM pod, two inert Mk 84 bombs, and two external tanks. In February 1994, this Fighting Falcon was with the 56th Fighter Wing, Air Education and Training Command, at Luke AFB, Arizona. (René J. Francillon)

Main wheels rotating into fuselage recesses and nose gear retracting aft, a F-16C Block 30 competes for the 347th FW in Gunsmoke '94. (Jim Dunn)

A LANTIRN-equipped Block 40 Fighting Falcon from the 421st FS, 388th FW, gets in position beneath a KC-135E to take on fuel during a training sortie over northern Arizona and southern Utah on 22 April 1993. (René J. Francillon)

The USAF Air Demonstration Team received its first F-16 on 22 June 1982 but did not complete its conversion from T-38As to F-16As until the spring of 1985. F-16Cs have now replaced F-16As as primary demonstration aircraft for the Thunderbirds. (Jim Dunn)

At peak strength in the late eighties, the Kansas ANG kept three squadrons of the 184th TFG at McConnell AFB busy training F-16 pilots for other ANG units. Now that training needs have been drastically reduced, two of these squadrons (the 161st and 177th) are being inactivated while the third (the 127th) is converting to B-1Bs. (Carl E. Porter)

Carrying the LF tail code of the 58th TTW, and the black-bordered yellow fin stripe of the 314th TFTS, 84-0323 taxies below the tower at Hill AFB, Utah, on 20 July 1988. (René J. Francillon)

How better to evoke the midwest in an aviation book than by showing an aircraft taxiing in the midst of a corn field? The 162d FS, 178th FG, Ohio ANG, at Springfield-Beckley MAP converted from A-7D/Ks to F-16C/D Block 30s in 1993. (Douglas D. Olson)

Photographed at McChord AFB, Washington, in June 1994, this LANTIRN-equipped Block 40 F-16D belongs to the 74th FS, 23d Wing, at Pope AFB, North Carolina. (Jim Dunn)

In April 1989, seven months before the fall of the Berlin Wall, the 64th Aggressor Squadron at Nellis AFB completed its conversion from F-5E/Fs to F-16C/Ds and plans to assign Fighting Falcons to aggressor squadrons with USAFE, the 527th AS at RAF Bentwaters, and PACAF, the 26th AS at Kadena AB, proceeded apace. However, the end of the Cold War soon eliminated most of the aggressor requirements. (René J. Francillon)

Landing at McClellan AFB, California, on 24 May 1991, this Nellis-based aggressor was by that time assigned to the Adversary Tactics Division of the 4440th Tactical Fighter Training Group as the 64th Aggressor Squadron had been inactivated on 5 October 1990. (Jim Dunn)

Pilot and crew chief from the Adversary Tactics Division prepare for a sortie in the afternoon of 17 February 1993. (René J. Francillon)

Gear almost in the wells, a pair of ATD aggressors are on their way to 'boogieing' over the Nellis range in October 1993. The tail code WA was first assigned in 1968 to the 4525th Fighter Weapons Wing in accordance with AFM66-1. The abbreviation ATD came into being after the inactivation of the 64th Aggressor Squadron. (Jim Dunn)

Aggressive tails: Three F-16Cs and a F-16D of the Adversary Tactics Division at parade rest on the sprawling ramp of Nellis AFB. (René J. Francillon)

86-0041, a two-seat Block 32 aggressor, on final approach at Nellis AFB in June 1991. (Jim Dunn)

After competitive evaluation, the Lockheed YF-22 version powered by Pratt & Whitney YF119 engines was selected in April 1991 as the intended replacement for air superiority versions of the F-15. Losing competitors were the GE-powered version of the YF-22 and P&W- and GE-powered versions of the Northrop YF-23. (Lockheed)

Reducing the force quantitatively while threats remain both numerous and diverse means that the Armed Forces will have to rely on qualitative improvements. Hence, the Air Force will be very much dependent on continued development and procurement of the F-22 Rapier. (Lockheed)

The F-22 will offer significant improvements over the F-15. Notably, carrying air-to-air missiles in internal weapons bay instead of externally as has been the case with most recent fighters, the Rapier will be significantly stealthier and will be capable of sustained supersonic cruise without having to use fuel-guzzling afterburners. (Lockheed)

First USAF fighter capable of supersonic speeds in level flight, the Super Sabre was first assigned to the 479th Fighter-Day Wing in September 1954 and was last used in its intended role by the 113th TFS of the Indiana ANG. Fourteen years after the Terre Haute unit had sent its last F-100Ds to storage at MASDC in November 1979, the last QF-100 drones were expended. (Jim Dunn)

In January 1988, the USAF still carried 193 Super Sabres in its inventory. Flight Systems, Inc, at Mojave had one F-100F and 14 F-100Ds for drone conversions (including 56-3053 photographed at Tyndall AFB in October 1988 after it had been droned), 19 QF-100Ds, and one QF-100F. The 475th Weapons Group at Tyndall AFB had five F-100Ds, 41 QF-100Ds, one F-100F, and two QF-100Fs. At Davis-Monthan AFB, MASDC stored 48 F-100Ds and 61 F-100Fs. Seventy-three months later, there were only four F-100Ds and 11 F-100Fs stored at AMARC to await sale to smelters. (Jim Dunn)

56-3861 of the 475th Weapons Group at Tyndall AFB on 19 October 1988. By then, this F-100F had logged some 6,200 hours. (Jim Dunn)

In January 1988, the 119th FIS, New Jersey ANG, was flying the last Delta Dart interceptors (14 F-106As, including 59-0023 which had logged 7,303 by the end of January 1988, and two F-106Bs). Two As and three Bs were bailed to Rockwell. In addition, the Air Force had 140 F-106As and 29 F-106Bs in storage or awaiting conversion as QF-106 drones, five QF-106As, and two QF-106Bs. (Jim Dunn)

The last Delta Dart to be modified as a drone was flown in July 1994 from AMARC to American Electronics Laboratory's Aero Division near St Louis to be fitted with telemetry and remote control equipment. Belonging to the 475th Weapons Group at Tyndall AFB, this pair of QF-106 drones was photographed in October 1988. (Jim Dunn)

57-2513 was one of three F-106Bs bailed to Rockwell for use as B-1B chase plane at Air Force Plant 42 in Palmdale. This 30 October 1988 photo was taken at this California facility. (Peter B. Lewis)

67-0070, a F-111A of the 366th TFW at Mountain Home AFB Idaho, wears the yellow fin cap identifying aircraft assigned to the 389th TFTS. The wing retired its F-111As in the spring of 1992. (René J. Francillon)

In January 1993, 31 F-111As were stored at AMARC, but 67-0050 was still with SM-ALC at McClellan AFB. The high-time F-111A, 67-0108, logged 5,717 hours before being stored, a rather remarkable figure for an aircraft designed to operate in the high-stress environment of low-level flying. (René J. Francillon)

SM tail code was first carried by aircraft assigned to SM-ALC (Sacramento Air Logistics Center) during the spring of 1991. 67-0075 was photographed on approach to McClellan AFB on 21 May 1991. (Jim Dunn)

The F-111D, the most advanced tactical strike Aardvark, entered service with the 4427th TFTS, 27th TFW, in November 1971. Briefly carrying the CE tail code of this training squadron, F-111Ds mostly carried CC tail code while serving with squadrons of the 27th TFW (those of the 523d TFS, including 68-0163 photographed at Nellis AFB on 24 June 1992, being distinguished by their blue fin cap). The last F-111Ds were stored at AMARC in 1992. (René J. Francillon)

Off to work we go: 68-095 of the 522d TFS roars off runway 3 Left at Nellis AFB on 18 September 1991 carrying Mk 82 bombs on wing racks and AN/ALQ-131 ECM pod on the rear fuselage station. (René J. Francillon)

Coded WA, 68-0086 was assigned to the 431st Test Squadron at McClellan AFB when photographed at this California base in January 1991. (Jim Dunn)

Although F-111Es served briefly and in smaller number with other units, the E version of the Aardvark will best be remembered for its 23-year service with the 20th TFW at RAF Upper Heyford. F-111Es were first assigned to this Oxfordshire base in September 1970 and were with the 20th Fighter Wing until its disbandment in 1993. (Carl E. Porter)

Stabilator fully depressed and pilot standing on the brakes, 67-0120 of the 27th TFW is ready to takeoff from runway 3 Left at Nellis AFB on 15 March 1990 during Red Flag 90-2. (René J. Francillon)

Wearing the red fin cap of the 77th FS, 68-0046 was photographed in England some 15 months before the squadron was deactivated. Before being stored at AMARC, this F-111D had logged 5,291 flight hours. (Michael Gruenenfelder)

Carrying inert Paveway guided bombs on wing stations and AN/AVQ-26 Pave Tack in the forward weapons bay, 70-2400, a F-111F of the 431st Test Squadron, returns to its home base at McClellan AFB in November 1990. On 28 February 1994, this F-111F was carried in the inventory of the 46th Test Wing at Eglin AFB, Florida. (Jim Dunn)

On its way from its home at Cannon AFB, New Mexico, to the Wendover Bombing and Gunnery Range in northern Utah, this F-111F of the 27th Fighter Wing pulls away from a KC-135E of the Pennsylvania ANG during an April 1993 training sortie. (Jim Dunn)

A F-111F of the 524th FS moves into position to take on fuel from a KC-10A of the 79th ARS during a sortie over eastern Nevada on 19 May 1993. (René J. Francillon)

On take-off, the combination main landing gear door/air brake of the F-111 deploys and creates drag. That critical moment was captured on film as this Aardvark from the 522d FS struggles to gain height after lifting off from runway 3 Left at Nellis AFB on its way to the range during Gunsmoke '93. (Jim Dunn)

Off we go into the wild blue yonder: Carrying a light load of inert bombs, a F-111F from the 522d FS, 27th FW, has no difficulties climbing away from the runway in full burner. (Jim Dunn)

Both Aardvark and Warthog undergo PDM at SM-ALC. Photographed on the ramp at McClellean AFB before being returned to service are 72-1444, a F-111F from the 46th Test Wing which had logged 5,088 hours by 28 February 1944, and 80-0263, an A-10A with 4,212 hours on its log just overhauled for the 110th FG, Michigan ANG. (Jim Dunn)

Fifteen of the 23 F-111Gs stored at AMARC at the beginning of 1994 are getting a new lease on life as they have been acquired by the Royal Australian Air Force as F-111C attrition replacements and as sources of spare parts for aircraft assigned to No 82 Wing at RAAF Amberley, Queensland. (René J. Francillon)

On 28 February 1994, five months after being photographed in the markings of the 2874th Test Squadron, 68-0247 had joined 22 other F-111Gs stored at AMARC. (Carl E. Porter)

Assigned to the 431st Test Squadron at McClellan AFB, California, this F-111G was photographed at NAS Fallon, Nevada, on 26 September 1991. Later assigned to the 27th FW at Cannon AFB, New Mexico, 68-0274 crashed in 1993. (René J. Francillon)

66-0013, one of two EF-111As initially assigned to Det 3, 4485th Test Squadron. Although the squadron was assigned to the Tactical Air Warfare Center (hence the OT tail code) at Eglin AFB, Florida, its Det 3 operated first from Mountain Home AFB, Idaho, and then from Cannon AFB, New Mexico, to benefit from maintenance support at these EF-111 operational bases. (Jim Dunn)

Taxiing back to the ramp at Mountain Home AFB, 66-0051 from the 390th ECS, 366th TFW, was photographed at the Idaho base on 18 July 1988. (René J. Francillon)

During Desert Storm, EF-111As from the 42d ECS, USAFE, and the 390th ECS, TAC, were assigned to the 48th TFW (Provisional) at Taif AB, Saudi Arabia, and to the 7440th TFW (Provisional) at Incirlik AB, Turkey, to provide much needed, and very effective, SEAD (Suppression of Enemy Air Defenses). This veteran of 49 Desert Storm sorties (a better than one a day average) was photographed at SM-ALC in April 1991. (Jim Dunn)

Photographed at Chièvres, Belgium, on 30 August 1991, 66-0055 from the 42d ECS, 66th ECW, was one of five EF-111As which during Desert Storm had flown combat sorties over Iraq while assigned to the 7440th TFW (Provisional) at Incirlik AB, Turkey. (Jean Soenen)

Concern over Saddam Hussein's intentions necessitates maintaining not insignificant forces in Saudi Arabia. Detached from the 27th FW at Cannon AFB, New Mexico, to the 4404th Composite Wing at Dhahran RSAFB, this EF-111A was photographed at this Saudi base in early 1994. (N. Donald)

With the inactivation of the 20th FW and 66th ECW and the conversion of the 48th FW and 366th Wing to other aircraft all operational Aardvarks and 'Sparkvarks' are now with the 27th FW at Cannon AFB. On 28 February 1994, the 27th FW was assigned 24 F-111Es, 78 F-111Fs, and 39 EF-111As, including aircraft undergoing PDM at the Sacramento Air Logistics Center. (Jim Dunn)

Left and below: A total of 76 FB-111As were procured for SAC. Most served with the 380th Bomb Wing at Plattsburgh AFB, New York, between 1971 and 1991, and with the 509th Bomb Wing at Pease AFB, New Hampshire, between 1970 and 1990. 'A Wingan' 10 Prayers' (68-0278) last saw operational duty with the 380th BW. Subsequently modified to F-111G standard and serving with the 27th TFW/27th FW, it was stored at AMARC after logging 6,630 flight hours. (Jim Dunn)

Permanently assigned to the Sacramento Air Logistics Center, 67-0159 received this spectacular scheme in 1984. After being withdrawn, this FB-111A was placed on display at the McClellan Aviation Museum where it was photographed in December 1991. (Jim Dunn)

Following public unveiling at Nellis AFB on 21 April 1990, F-117As were sent to numerous air shows and open houses during the summer and fall of 1990, including one held at Beale AFB, California, during which 80-0789 was photographed on 9 November 1990. By that time, 18 F-117As from the 415th TFS were already at King Khalid AB, Taif, Saudi Arabia, ready to teach senior Iraqi officers to do the rock 'n' roll in their headquarters and deep shelters. (Peter B. Lewis)

Bearing the TR tail code assigned to the 37th TFW when it was based at Tonopah Test Range, 85-0818 is about to touch down on runway 16 at McClellan AFB on 21 May 1991. (Jim Dunn)

79-10783, the fourth full-scale development YF-117A at McClellan AFB on 24 May 1991. Taken from the control tower as the aircraft taxies away, this view provides good detail of exhaust and drag chute housing. (Jim Dunn)

McClellan AFB, 24 May 1991: Barely visible at the top of the starboard vertical tail surface of 79-10783 is the tail code ED, indicating that this YF-117A was assigned to the 6510th Test Wing at Edwards AFB. (Jim Dunn)

Effective but inelegant, the multi-faceted airframe of the Nighthawk is likely to remain unique as advances in LO (low observable) technology is enabling a welcome return to more aerodynamic designs. 82-0800 was photographed at Castle AFB, California, on 5 October 1991. (Jim Dunn)

85-0813 from the 417th FS, 49th FW, towed below the control tower at Kingsley Field, Klamath Falls, Oregon in August 1993. Since F-117As were transferred to the 49th FW at Holloman AFB, New Mexico, it has proven increasingly difficult to maintain their radar absorbent finish due to the need to park the Nighthawks in the open as the New Mexico base, unlike the Tonopah facility, lacks hangars. (Carl E. Porter)

Nine TG-7A motor gliders are in service at the Air Force Academy for flight familiarization. They carry both civil registrations and Air Force serials as illustrated by 87-0761, aka N765AF. (S.S. Hampton, USAF)

Dual civil registration/military serial number are also carried by T-41s of the Air Force Academy. On 28 February 1994, there still were 48 T-41Cs and two T-41Ds at the Academy. (Paul Negri)

The acquisition of Slingsby T-3As to replace Cessna T-41s is a sad commentary on the state to which frivolous lawsuits have brought the once dominant US light aircraft industry and its three giants: Beech, Cessna, and Piper. The T-3, in which most future USAF pilots will receive flight familiarization, is a British-built development of a French design. Did we hear politicians deplore unemployment in the aircraft industry before voting themselves large pay raises? (USAF)

On 31 January 1988, 69-6616 was assigned to the 1st Helicopter Squadron at Andrews AFB, Maryland. Five and a half months later, this UH-1N was photographed at Fairchild AFB, Washington, where it was operated by Det 24 of the 40th Aerospace Rescue and Recovery Squadron, Military Airlift Command, in support of basic and advanced survival courses run by the 3614th Combat Crew Training Wing. (Christian Jacquet)

Sharing the helicopter ramp at Fairchild AFB with 69-6616, 69-6641 was finished in a scheme far less appropriate to covert-type operations flown in support of survival courses. (Christian Jacquet)

Better suited to VIP operations, this blue and gold scheme with white top was worn by 69-6619 photographed at Toul-Rosières AB, France, in July 1989. By the end of February 1994, the Air Force helicopter fleet still included four single-engine HH-1Hs and 66 twin-engine UH-1Ns. Five single-engine UH-1Fs were stored at McClellan AFB. (Christian Jacquet)

69-5802 of the 71st Aerospace Rescue and Recovery Squadron at Elmendorf AFB had logged 8,501 flight hours by the end of January 1988, a remarkable achievement for any helicopter and more so for one operating in the harsh Alaskan environment. (Carl E. Porter)

Also assigned to the 71st ARRS, this Jolly Green helicopter practices hover close to the ground at Elmendorf AFB with the cloud-shrouded Chugach Mountains in the background. (Carl E. Porter)

Air refueling probe fully extended and almost safely in the HC-130P port basket, a HH-3E from the 129th ARRS, California ANG, gets some air refueling practice off the coast of northern California, near Half Moon Bay. (René J. Francillon)

Like fish out of water: PJs (parachute rescue jumpers) of the 129th ARRS being winched out of Lake Berryessa, California. This California ANG squadron converted from HH-3Es to HH-60Gs during the fall of 1990. (René J. Francillon)

In February 1994, the Air Force still had nine HH-3Es, five with the 41st RQS at Patrick AFB, Florida, and four with the 33d RQS at Kadena AB, Okinawa. By the end of the year, these last Jolly Greens had joined three CH-3Es and 15 HH-3Es stored at AMARC. Less than six years after it had been photographed when serving with the 102d ARRS, New York ANG, 69-5805 was no longer in the inventory. (Tom Kaminski)

HH-3E of the 1550th FTS being refueled by a HC-130P of the 1551st FTS over the Rio Grande Valley on 29 April 1989. After the air refueling portion of the flight was completed, the HC-130P proceeded to do four hours of tactical flying in and out of canyons in northern New Mexico. Admittedly, the photographer's face turned Jolly Green's green. Decorum was preserved as the photographer did not toss his cookies! (René J. Francillon)

Eight HH-53Bs, distinguished by bracing struts supporting external tanks, were built for the Air Force and were assigned serials 66-14428 to 66-14435. In January 1988, three HH-53Bs were still operational, one was being brought up to MH-53H standard, and one had already been modified as a MH-53H. Having been brought up to MH-53J standard, five of these helicopters (66-14428, 66-14429, and 66-14431/14433) were still in service in February 1994, with the high-time aircraft having logged 9,067 hours. (Carl E. Porter)

In January 1988, the last three operational HH-53Bs were with the 1st SOW at Eglin Auxiliary Field #9 and with the 1550th CCTW at Kirtland AFB. (Carl E. Porter)

As MH-53Js have logged between 5,126 and 9,067 flight hours by the end of February 1994, the Air Force cannot afford using these much-needed special operations helicopters to provide type conversion training. This need had been anticipated as far back as 1988 and, accordingly, six CH-53As were acquired from the Marine Corps for use as TH-53A trainers with the 1550th CCTW (later redesignated the 542d Crew Training Wing) at Kirtland AFB, New Mexico. (René J. Francillon)

By February 1994, all Air Force-procured HH-53s remaining in the inventory had been modified to MH-53J standard. Twenty-seven were with the 20th SOS at Hurlburt Field, Florida; five were with the 21st SOS at RAF Alconbury, England; five were with the 31st SOS at Osan AB, Korea; and four with the 542d CTW at Kirtland AFB, New Mexico. (USAF)

Never particularly clean, the H-53 has grown many warts, bumps, and lumps as it grew older. In its MH-53J configuration it is now replete with protuberances, including air refueling probe, radome for AN/APQ-158 terrain-following radar, and AN/AAQ-10 FLIR turret. (USAF)

Covert infil-exfil is the life blood of special operations. Far from ending the need for such activities, the end of the Cold War created new requirements, particularly in support of hostage rescue operations. Communism may be dead, but crazies still abound. (USAF)

Playing hide-and-seek in San Francisco Bay fog, a HH-60G from the 129th ARRS, California ANG, transits from its home at NAS Moffett Field to the training area off Half Moon Bay on 28 May 1991. (René J. Francillon)

Supporters of the Air National Guard are dismayed by the current generic look of Guard aircraft and helicopters, and people. 'Total Force' is a powerful political motto, but many regret the proud days of the California Guard, the New York Guard, or the Wyoming Guard. Sameness and political correctness breed banality. What is that thing wearing a fatigue? Is that a he or a she? Is that person Air Force, Guard, squid, or jarhead? Why can't military personnel be allowed to be proud of their unit? (René J. Francillon)

California's earthquake country: 88-26115, call sign 'King 15,' flies off Point Reyes National Seashore with fault-born Tomales Bay in the background. (René J. Francillon)

Acquisition of Blackhawk derivatives by the Air Force was long delayed as development of HH-60A, HH-60D, and HH-60E variants ran into budgetary difficulties. Finally, MH-60Gs for special operations units and HH-60Gs for ANG (including 88-26113 of the 102d Air Rescue Squadron, New York ANG) and AFRES units became operational at the beginning of the nineties. (Stéphane Meunier)

Having to operate from snow-covered surfaces on a regular basis, HH-60Gs of the 210th Air Rescue Squadron, Alaska ANG, are fitted with skis. 88-26105 was photographed at Kulis ANGB, Anchorage IAP, in July 1991. (Edric G. Francillon)

A MH-60G of the 55th SOS slides into position behind a HC-130 tanker of the 9th SOS. (TSgt Kit Thompson, USAF)

Ever since President Johnson revealed on 29 February 1964 that 'the performance of the A-11 far exceeds that of any other aircraft in the world,' the Lockheed Blackbird series – comprised of the A-12 for the Central Intelligence Agency and the YF-12 and SR-71 for the Air Force – has held a special fascination for aviation buffs and others. 64-17976 was photographed at the boom over Idaho on 28 September 1989, four months before the official retirement of this Mach 3+ reconnaissance aircraft. (René J. Francillon)

Back from its 28 September 1989 training sortie, 64-17976 receives post-flight servicing at Beale AFB. That scene will again be seen if Congress, which during the summer of 1994 voted funds to restore three SR-71As to USAF service, prevails over the Air Force. (René J. Francillon)

When USAF aircraft again began displaying nose art, SR-71s gained tail art. That sported by 64-17976 was rather discrete but nevertheless attractive. (René J. Francillon)

When fully fueled before a mission, the SR-71 appeared to be on the edge of serious trouble as low-volatility JP-7 leaked abundantly. Pools of fuel are seen on the hangar floor as engines are started prior to 64-17968 departing for a training sortie on 27 September 1989. (René J. Francillon)

Beale AFB, 26 January 1990: The 9th Strategic Reconnaissance Wing publicly bids goodbye to the SR-71. Of the 32 SR-71s built by Lockheed (64-17950 to 64-17981), 12 had been written off and seven had been withdrawn prior to 1990, but 12 SR-71As and one SR-71B were still either in service, undergoing overhaul, or stored in Palmdale when the Air Force (first?) retired its Blackbird. (René J. Francillon)

Blackbird, indeed: The unique fuselage/wing/power plant blending of the SR-71A is silhouetted against clear blue sky during a display at Beale AFB. (Carl E. Porter)

Add propellers and you could almost get another Ford Trimotor! From this angle, the TR-1A with extended nose to house the Precision Location Strike System (PLSS) and super pods takes on a rather odd appearance. (Carl E. Porter)

Caught in tangent light conditions on take-off at Beale AFB, 80-1074 shows off its Q-bay camera port beneath the forward fuselage. TR-1As remaining in the Air Force inventory have been redesignated U-2Rs. (Carl E. Porter)

Photographed at Beale AFB on 27 October 1991, 80-1084 is finished in the last scheme applied by SAC to TR-1As and U-2Rs. In service with ACC since June 1992, single-seat U-2Rs and two-set U-2RTs have added the tail code BB. It is worth noting that the Air Force, which releases serial numbers and flight hours for the F-117A and the B-2A, has never released similar information for the U-2 and the SR-71. Do you care to draw a conclusion? (Jim Dunn)

Activated in July 1941, 'Willie' was for over 52 years a major training base. A BRAC victim, Williams AFB, Arizona, was closed in October 1993. Its 82d Flying Training Wing had been comprised of the 96th FTS with T-37Bs and 97th FTS with T-38As. (René J. Francillon)

To enable SAC copilots to hone their skill by flying more hours than available while assigned to bombers or tankers, ATC provided Accelerated Copilot Enrichment detachments at all major SAC bases. Some ACE detachments were equipped with T-37Bs, others with T-38As. This T-37B of the 323d FTW at Mather AFB was assigned to the ACE detachment at Fairchild AFB, Washington, for use by KC-135A and B-52H copilots of the 92d BMW. (Christian Jacquet)

Bearing the code NT (for Navigation Training), this T-37B shooting an approach at Castle AFB on 2 November 1992 is identified as a Tweetie Bird assigned to the 454th FTS, 323d FTW, at nearby Mather AFB. Both of these California bases are now closed. (René J. Francillon)

The 479th Tactical Training Wing was activated on 1 January 1977 at Holloman AFB, New Mexico, to provide LIFT (Lead-in Fighter Training) to recent pilot and navigator training graduates. At peak strength, its four tactical fighter training squadrons – 433d (Satan's Angels), 434th (Red Devils), 435th (Black Eagles), and 436th (Black Aces) – were assigned 113 AT-38Bs and flew more than 35,000 sorties per year. By 28 February 1994, only 66 AT-38Bs remained operational and were assigned by ACC to the 49th FW and by AETC to various FTWs (with which they serve alongside with T-38As) (René J. Francillon)

Force drawdown and the resultant reduction in number of new pilots needed by the Air Force have had a drastic impact on the T-38. Before the Soviet collapse, when pilot requirements were at near record peacetime levels, the Air Force worried that, due to aging of the fleet, it would not have enough T-38s. Accordingly, it wanted to get back all Talons loaned to other US and foreign operators. Now T-38s are again plentiful and USAF can afford loaning 40 Talons to Taiwan pending delivery of F-16s to the Republic of China Air Force. (René J. Francillon)

The 80th FTW at Sheppard AFB, Texas, has provided undergraduate training for NATO pilots for many years, hence the stylized NATO star on the fin of this T-38A.

Carrying the fin band which identified aircraft assigned to the 9th Strategic Reconnaissance Wing at Beale AFB, California, 64-13217 was photographed at touchdown in March 1991. (Jim Dunn)

Wearing the tail band of the 64th FTW at Reese AFB, 62-3701 of the 54th FTS comes in to land at Nellis AFB on 18 September 1991. (René J. Francillon)

To supplement its F-117A, the 37th TFW inherited A-7Ds and A-7Ks from the 4450th Tactical Group. It later replaced its Corsair IIs with AT-38Bs as shown by 65-10382 carrying the TR tail code of the Tonopah unit. (Jim Dunn)

The USAF Test Pilot School at Edwards AFB gets much use from its fleet of ED-coded T-38As. On 28 February 1994, 17 T-38As were assigned to the 445th Test Squadron, 412th Test Wing, including 67-14943 which by then had logged 8,347 hours. (Jim Dunn)

The XL 'Extra Large' tail code is assigned to the 47th FTW at Laughlin AFB, Texas. In 1994, the 47th had three flying squadrons, the 85th with Cessna T-37Bs, the 86th with Beech T-1As, and the 87th with Northrop T-38As and AT-38Bs. (René J. Francillon)

Talons assigned as companion trainers to ACC units are now finished in the same scheme as the parent unit's operational aircraft. Hence, T-38As of the 7th FS – the F-117 RTU at Holloman AFB, New Mexico – have a black finish like Nighthawks of the 49th Fighter Wing. This photo of 65-10376 taken at Travis AFB, California, in October 1994 is noteworthy as, unlike the wing's F-117As, this Talon has high gloss wings and fuselage; tail surfaces, however, have a matte finish. (Jim Dunn)

Developed from the very successful Boeing 737 jetliner, the T-43A was ordered by the Air Force in 1971 as a navigation trainer to replace the Convair T-29. Most went to the 323d FTW at Mather AFB but, beginning in 1978, two T-43As were assigned to Detachment 1, HQ, Colorado ANG, to provide instruction and training on the principles of celestial, inertial, radar, and radio navigation to cadets at the Air Force Academy. Later, the Colorado unit added two transport-configured CT-43As. (René J. Francillon)

Before closure of Mather AFB and inactivation of the 454th FTS, 323d FTW, T-43As of the 454th FTS briefly wore NT tail code. T-43A navigation trainers are now operated by the 558th FTS, 12th FTW, at Randolph AFB, and are coded RA. (Jim Dunn)

Detachment 1, HQ, Colorado ANG, was redesignated the 200th Airlift Squadron on 15 March 1992. Soon afterward, 72-0287 was photographed at Buckley ANGB, Colorado, in this smart new scheme. (Douglas D. Olson)

Once we were out of Southeast Asia, the need for a specialized COIN aircraft disappeared rapidly. With the Air Force, OV-10As were then used exclusively in the FAC role. In an all-out war against an enemy with a sophisticated air defense system, the twin-boom, turboprop-powered would have had a low survivability rate (as the Marines found out with their OV-10Ds during the Gulf War). (René J. Francillon)

Based at Eielson AFB, Alaska, the 25th Tactical Air Support Squadron, 343d Composite Wing, flew OV-10As between 1986 and 1989. 67-14630 was photographed in Alaska on 24 July 1988. (Robert S. Hopkins III)

67-14654 of the 22d Tactical Air Support Training Squadron photographed on final approach to McClellan AFB on 30 March 1990. It is worth noting that when they were no longer found suitable for service with active duty units, OV-10As were not among types dumped on AFRES and/or ANG units. (Jim Dunn)

When the Air Force replaced its last O-2 FAC aircraft with OV-10As, a few found unexpected customers. 67-21414, photographed at NAS Fallon, Nevada, in June 1989, was one of the ex-USAF O-2As flown by VFA-125 to mark targets for naval strike trainees and to patrol the Fallon bombing range. (René J. Francillon)

Unlike its predecessors from de Havilland Canada – the L-20/U-6 Beaver, the U-1 Otter, and the AC-1/CV-2/C-7 Caribou, the rather outstanding DHC-6 Twin Otter did not attract much interest from the US Armed Forces. Six UV-18A were acquired for the Alaska Army Air National Guard and two UV-18Bs were acquired for parachute training at the Air Force Academy. Like other aircraft of the Air Force Academy, they carry dual civilian/military identifications, that illustrated being N70464/77-0464. (Robert B. Greby)

As an introduction to the following pages devoted to tail shots, we start with this confusing message: Back from the Gulf War, 64-047 displays both the tail code BH of the Birmingham-based 106th TRS and the 'High Rollers' fin band of the Reno-based 192d TRS. Belonging to the Alabama ANG unit and flown by it to Bahrein during Desert Shield, this RF-4C-22-MC was serviced and flown by Nevada guardsmen during Desert Storm. (René J. Francillon)

59-2593, B-52G
441st BMS, 320th BMW, SAC
@ Mather AFB, January 1988. (René J. Francillon)

64-0911, F-4C
114th TFTS, OR ANG
@ Kingsley Field, July 1988. (René J. Francillon)

57-2335, T-37B
ACE detachment, 323d FTW, ATC
@ Fairchild AFB, July 1988 . (René J. Francillon)

57-1430, KC-135A
43d & 92d AREFS, 92nd BMW, SAC
@ Fairchild AFB, July 1988. (Christian Jacquet)

80-1082, TR-1A
99th SRS, 9th SRW, SAC
@ Beale AFB, August 1988. (Jim Dunn)

68-0123, F-111D
523d TFS, 27th TFW, TAC
@ Mather AFB, September 1988. (Jim Dunn)

86-0304, F-16C
80th TFS, 8th TFW, PACAF
@ Kadena AB, September 1988. (Robert S. Hopkins III)

63-7994, EC-135G
70th AREFS, 305th AREFW, SAC
@ Mather AFB, November 1988. (Jim Dunn)

64-1084, RF-4C, 45th TRTS, 67th TRW, TAC; 63-8112, AT-38B, 433d
TFTS, 479th TTW, TAC; 63-8112, F-111D, 523d TFS, 27th TFW,
TAC @ Mather AFB, November 1988. (Jim Dunn)

63-8175, AT-38B
479th TTW, 833d AD, TAC
@ Holloman AFB, May 1989. (René J. Francillon)

76-1607, E-3B
963d AWACS, 552d AWACW, TAC
@ Tinker AFB, May 1989. (René J. Francillon)

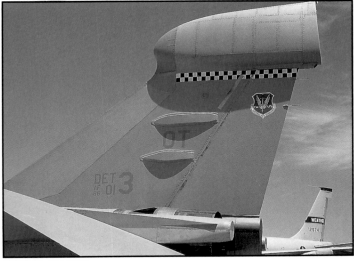

66-0013, EF-111A
Det 3, 4485th Test Squadron, AFSC
@ McClellan AFB, May 1989. (Jim Dunn)

65-9405, C-141B
514th MAW (Associate), AFRES
@ Pope AFB, June 1989. (René J. Francillon)

87-0195, F-15E
336th TFS, 4th TFW, TAC
@ Seymour Johnson AFB, June 1989. (René J. Francillon)

71-0377, A-7D
146th TFS, 112th TFG, PA ANG
@ Greater Pittsburgh IAP, June 1990. (René J. Francillon)

63-7783, EC-130E (Rivet Rider)
193d SOS, 193d SOG, PA ANG
@ Harrisburg IAP, June 1990. (René J. Francillon)

79-0088, A-10A
104th TFS, 175th TFG, MD ANG
@ Glenn L. Martin State AP, June 1990. (René J. Francillon)

62-4126, C-135B, and 85-6973, C-137C
1st MAS, 89th MAW, MAC
@ Andrews AFB, June 1990. (René J. Francillon)

76-0077, F-15A
123d FIS, 142d FIG, OR ANG
@ Portland IAP, August 1990. (René J. Francillon)

59-5957, C-130B
187th TAS, 153d TAG, WY ANG
@ Cheyenne MAP, October 1990. (Douglas D. Olson)

82-1041, F-16B
179th FIS, 148th FIG, MN ANG
@ Duluth IAP, October 1990. (Carol McKenzie)

86-0271, F-16C
ATD, 57th FWW, TAC
@ Nellis AFB, June 1991. (René J. Francillon)

56-3638, KC-135E
197th ARS, 161st ARG, AZ ANG
@ Sky Harbor IAP, May 1992. (René J. Francillon)

62-4132, RC-135W
38th RS, 55th Wing, ACC
@ Beale AFB, November 1992. (Jim Dunn)

69-0249, F-4G
190th FS, 124th FG, ID ANG
@ Gowen Field, May 1993. (René J. Francillon)

86-0135, B-1B
28th BS, 384th BG, ACC
@ Beale AFB, June 1993. (Jim Dunn)

62-1811, C-130E
115th AS, 146th AW, CA ANG
@ Schoonover Field, June 1994. (René J. Francillon)

90-0533, C-17A
437th AW, AMC, and 315th AW (Associate), AFRES
@ McChord AFB, June 1994. (René J. Francillon)

86-0030, KC-10A
4th Wing, ACC, and 916th ARG, AFRES
@ McChord AFB, June 1994. (René J. Francillon)

68-0219, C-5A
337th AS, 439th AW, AFRES
@ Travis AFB, August 1994. (René J. Francillon)

Also from the publisher

McDONNELL-DOUGLAS
F-15 EAGLE
A PHOTO CHRONICLE
BILL HOLDER & MIKE WALLACE
FOREWORD BY GENERAL JOHN M. LOH
COMMANDER AIR COMBAT COMMAND

PHANTOM
IN COMBAT
WALTER J. BOYNE

This new photo chronicle covers the F-15 Eagle from its planning and development, to its success in Operation Desert Storm and post-Desert Storm operations in over 170 photographs, most in color. All types are covered, including foreign – Israel, Japan and Saudi Arabia – and the Strike Eagle.

Bill Holder is a retired USAF aero-space engineer, and is now a freelance writer specializing in aviation and automotive subjects. He lives in Dayton, OH. Mike Wallace has more than 22 years of Air Force public relations experience, and has been attached to Aeronautical Systems Division at Wright-Patterson AFB. He lives in Lewisburg, OH.

Phantom in Combat puts you in the cockpit with the missile-age aces as they fight for their lives in the skies of Vietnam and the Middle East. Providing a rich background to this testimony is a wealth of rare material. Here is the human face of modern air warfare, described by the commanders and crews who earned for the Phantom its reputation as the world's finest fighting aircraft.

Size: 8 1/2" x 11" over 150 color & b/w photographs
88 pages, soft cover
ISBN: 0-88740-662-9 $19.95

Size: 8 1/2" x 11" over 300 color & b/w photographs, charts, diagrams
192 pages, hard cover
ISBN: 0-88740-599-1 $35.00